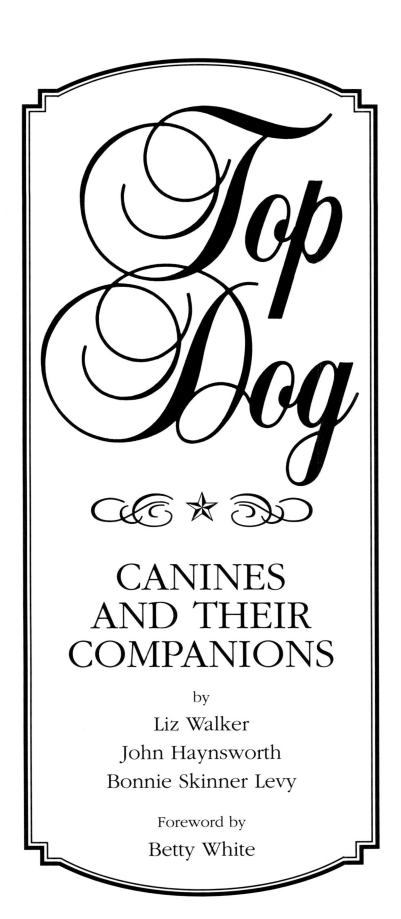

Top Dog

CANINES AND THEIR COMPANIONS

by

Liz Walker

John Haynsworth

Bonnie Skinner Levy

Foreword by

Betty White

Beautiful America Publishing Company

Beautiful America Publishing Company©
P.O. Box 646
Wilsonville, Oregon 97070

Library of Congress Catalog Number 91-769
ISBN 0-89802-571-0

Design: Jacelen Pete and Michael Brugman
Editing: Andrea Tronslin and Donald Beckett II
Linotronic output: LeFont Typography
Printed in Hong Kong

This book is dedicated to
that indescribable blend of total
loyalty,
affection,
acceptance,
and love...
that is the very nature of dogs,
and is the inspiration for this book.

Table of Contents

List of Canines & Companions

List of Canines

Acknowledgments

This book would not have been possible without...Mr. James Wharton, our dear friend and guardian angel whose constant guidance was invaluable...Mr. Roger Horchow for his unwavering support from the very start to the finish of our happy project...Pam Evans and Happy Tails Pet Boutique for their fabulous gift baskets overflowing with the canine treats that kept our four-legged participants quite happy...Betty White, a woman whose warm acceptance helped put *TOP DOG* on the map...Ed Lazano for his witty ways, L.A. driving skills and expert photographic techniques...Ted and Beverly Paul for their gutsy move to take on three Texas authors, their strict adherance to quality, and their openness to ideas...Jeffrey Lane, for his enthusiastic embrace of our project, his unique creativity, and the elegance he adds to everything he becomes a part of...Jan Miller, for saying "yes" to be our agent on the sheer instinct that *TOP DOG* was a winner...Lester Levy Jr., for sharing his entrepreneurial skills, business ideas, and last but certainly not least, his house in La Jolla...Denise Haynsworth, for sharing her talented husband with *TOP DOG*...and, finally, a special thanks to Stuart Jacobson, a friend, a guide, a man to be remembered.

We also want to thank: Susie Jenkins, Danielle Johnston, Gianna DePaul, and the Haynsworth Studio staff; the whole Beautiful America Publishing gang including Jacie Pete, Larry Miller, and Andrea Tronslin; Ms. Ellen Terry; Mr. and Mrs. Wallace Skinner; Mr. Allan Knight; Mr. Armand Deutsch; Mr. Matthew Margolis; Mr. Irvin Levy; Mrs. Joan Schnitzer; Mr. Elijah Jones; Mr. John James; Mrs. Francis Martin, Jr.; Ms. Sylvia Ortega; Miss Mary Tyler Moore; Mr. Terry Simms; Mr. Charlie Corson; Ms. Martha Stewart; Mr. George W. Bush; Ms. Barbara Henckel; Ms. Gail Clark; Mr. Alan Peppard; Mr. Robert Fox; Mr. Harris L. Katleman; Ms. Sonya Stathis; Mr. Clarkson Hine; Ms. Elizabeth Sundance; Le Dufy Hotel; Matsushisa; The Rainbow Bar and Grill; The Chateau Marmount; Ms. Jonni Hartman; Mr. Dennis Ferrar; Ms. Felice Sands; Ms. Irene McDonald; Ms. Laura Danford; Mrs. Ruby Hamra; Ms. Terry Forst; Miss Chessie Hortenstine; Mr. Richard Grant; Ms. Christina Wyeth; Ms. Pamela Cropp; Mr. Sandy Friedman; Mr. Gary Gero; Ms. Kari Clark; Ms. Marinelle Guy; Mr. Gary Morton; and all of our fabulous *TOP DOG* participants who eagerly and joyously found time in their busy schedules to extol the many virtues of their favorite four-pawed friends.

"A person who has never owned a dog
has missed a wonderful part of life."

...Bob Barker

Foreword by Betty White

The invitation from Liz and Bonnie to write the foreword for this lovely book is an honor as well as a delightful surprise. Especially so, since many beloved personal friends are included in these pages. And there are some *people* I know in here, too.

Speaking from a human perspective, the famous faces in this volume make it an interesting conversation piece on any coffee table. Dogs, however, being the wise and perceptive creatures they are, couldn't care less that the people they live with happen to be celebrities...they simply love them for all the right reasons. Conversely, the length of a pedigree has nothing to do with being a *TOP DOG*.

The heated debate over which is best, the purebred dog vs. the canine of uncertain heritage, has been raging for centuries with no sign of letup in the foreseeable future. One could really take either side of that argument and come out a winner, for there are merits and minuses on both sides; it really distills down to individual preference. Personally, I would say the "best" dog is one with a leg on each corner if it weren't for a couple of outstanding three-legged exceptions I've met.

For anyone who loves surprises and enjoys guessing games, a mixed breed is probably ideal, particularly if little is known about the dog's background. The tiny big-footed puppy you expected to turn into a small terrier-type keeps growing into those feet until you find yourself with something of a wolfhound. Now you have the fun of guessing, "What else is in that dog?" It's a gamble but most of the time a happy one, and you've provided a home for a needy friend.

My Cricket was a six-week-old-foundling and the tiniest puppy I had ever seen. The classic catchall name for a variety of blends is "cockapoo," and at first I thought Crick was at least a "something-poo." It wasn't long, however, before his facial expression and demeanor left little doubt of a strong bichon frisé component. What the rest is I haven't figured out in seven years, nor do I care. He is perfect.

Purebreds, on the other hand, eliminate the guesswork. Throughout history the generic dog has been constantly redesigned according to specific human needs, until today worldwide there are upwards of some 350 breeds and counting. Whatever your pleasure...from Chihuahua to St. Bernard, Affenpinscher to Xoloitzcuintli...there are breeders who will deliver the custom-made dog to suit your temperament and lifestyle.

For me, there must always be a poodle in my life, whatever else is onboard. As a breed they are incredibly smart, achingly sweet-tempered and totally adaptable, and my small black Timothy has been all that and more for thirteen years.

The old saw about mutts being smarter is a myth, as genius dogs will turn up among both the mixed and the matched. Whichever your preference, the same holds true for a person/dog commitment as any other: you get back in direct proportion what you put into a relationship.

Enjoy these pages. The personal choices are enlightening, sometimes surprising, and always interesting. We already know, however, that the true *TOP DOGS* are our own.

Introduction

There are those who claim man was put on earth to give dog a best friend. Of course, these believers consist primarily of the four-pawed set, but whether man was created for the benefit of dog or vice versa is a moot point. From the campfire to the Jenn-Aire, these two have been inseparable, for better and for worse.

As President Lyndon Johnson once philosophized, "The fact that dogs haven't given up on humans completely and still make people their friends shows there must be some hope for the human race." Dogs have been tolerating the inconsistencies of *Homo sapiens* since the creation of man – there have been references to dogs whenever history has been recorded. In Iraq dog remains have been found beside human artifacts dating back 14,000 years, and man and dog have been sharing a unique and mutually beneficial relationship ever since.

Domestication occurred as soon as man and dog realized they needed each other. Man depended on his furry friend to guard his domain and help with the hunting, and dog came to rely on man because man knew how to cook and was willing to share his food. Plus, man carried around big spears to frighten off bullying beasts that liked to eat small dogs for lunch. It was a good relationship, marred only by the fact that dog gave more than he received. He contributed significantly to man's successes.

During the Stone Age, dogs were highly valued because they fought in battles, guarded temples and enabled their masters to capture dinner with a minimum of fuss. The Egyptians even worshipped their dogs, and Anubis, the Egyptian god of death, was depicted as a man with a dog-like head. When a dog died, the Egyptians would ceremoniously mummify its body and carry the remains in a solemn procession to the dog burial grounds. The whole household went into deep mourning.

Man's adoration of his new friend sometimes led to extreme behavior, as evidenced by the dog-loving Ethiopian tribesmen who once crowned a dog as king. The "king" showed his approval by wagging his tail, and his disapproval by barking. If he went so far as to lick your hand, you were assured a comfortable existence, but one growl could stand between you and your head. In China, little prince-like pooches lolled at the emperor's court, tended by eunuchs; their puppies were nursed by slaves whose children had been destroyed at birth. Death by torture was the penalty for raising a hand against a royal dog.

ven though these dogs of luxury were found among the elite from the Orient to the Mediterranean, during these early years most dogs worked for a living – it was over 3,000 years ago that an Athenian general wrote *Hunting With Dogs*. Both Greek poets and Roman authors delighted in stories about dogs, and the dog moralizes in many of Aesop's fables. In the ninth century B.C., Homer honored the dog's unswerving loyalty in *The Odyssey* when, after twenty years, Ulysses returns home disguised as a beggar and only Argos, his faithful hound, recognizes him. It is no wonder dogs are still referred to as "Fido," the Latin word for faithful. In ancient Rome, dogs were everywhere: hunting, fighting in the arenas, going to battle and guarding towns. Even Julius Caesar had a strong attachment to lap dogs.

During the sixteenth and seventeenth centuries, royalty had a big influence on the popularity of dogs. The French kings' dogs generally ran the palaces, and after King Henry III's spaniels accompanied him to church, they would cuddle up beside him in bed. He is credited with starting the fashion of keeping dogs as pets among royalty, and this tradition soon caught on with the British kings Charles I and II. In Queen Victoria's time, she was so crazy about her Pomeranians, rumor has it, that immediately after her coronation she returned home, stripped off her robes and set about bathing her favorite dog. Sixty-four years later, that Pomeranian's great-grandchild kept watch beside her on her deathbed.

In the twentieth century, English royalty continued this devotion, and the trend-setting Duke and Duchess of Windsor displayed their affection for their pugs by supplying them with mink and diamond collars, 14-karat Cartier leashes, and such delicacies as grilled capon breast and calves' liver, served in the pampered pups' engraved silver bowls.

oyalty is also credited with the onslaught of paintings portraying dogs, although dogs had been represented in art from the time man began to carve and draw. In prehistoric times, hunting scenes with dogs were carved on cave walls, and then Egyptians carved dogs on their tombs. With the possible exception of the horse, the dog has been portrayed on canvas more than any other animal.

Dogs were first depicted in Italian paintings as companions of saints. St. Francis of Assisi was a passionate animal lover, which accounts for the preponderance of dogs in Italian religious paintings. In France, Fragonard's canvases were filled with dogs, and then there was Jean Baptiste Oudry, whom Louis XV set up at the Louvre primarily to paint the palace dogs. Later, Henri Toulouse-Lautrec, who loved dogs, frequently used them in his posters and lithographs.

By the late Renaissance, the popularity of the dog had extended to all social classes, which accounts for the large number of Flemish, Dutch and German paintings depicting dogs with their merchant-class owners. Of course, it is the English who are most famous for painting canines; Sir Joshua Reynolds' and Thomas Gainsborough's works are filled with dogs, and Sir Edwin Landseer, who often painted Queen Victoria and her menagerie, gave his dogs human-like qualities.

During the late nineteenth century, painter Francis Barraud painted his black and white terrier, Nipper, peering inquisitively into the horn of a phonograph. The painting, *His Master's Voice*, was purchased by RCA and has become one of the world's most famous trademarks. Nipper's spotted face has appeared on record labels by the millions.

In America, dog paintings revolved primarily around the hunt. Percival Rosseau is probably the greatest American dog painter, and his *Diana Hunting* created quite a stir in the early 1900s because Diana's dog was accorded as much prominence as Diana. Americans have gleaned inspiration from the dog, resulting in many caricatures, satires and cartoons, from Walt Disney's *101 Dalmatians* to Charles Schultz's Snoopy.

anine characteristics have also been carved and sculpted – there are dog carvings from Babylonia dating from 1900 B.C. The Chinese molded dogs in bronze and the Romans chose marble to immortalize their canine elite. The dog has even been pictured on many noble crests through the years, as well as in the tapestries of the ancient Middle East, Asia and Pre-Columbian America.

Dogs have always been a favorite subject among writers. Who can forget Jack London's Buck or John Steinbeck's Charley? James Herriot continues the tradition with his heart-warming dog tales. Even Hollywood has been starring dogs in films since the silent era – often with top billing. Where would American cinema be without Rin Tin Tin, Lassie and Benji?

After the emphasis on hunting declined, the dog got to slack off a bit and function primarily as an affectionate companion, but, although many dogs hold a higher status than valued family members, dogs have pulled their own weight in the twentieth century. From the 40,000 dogs that fought in World War I to the teams of huskies that have rushed supplies across polar ice fields, the dog has certainly fulfilled his part of the bargain.

There are lead dogs for the physically impaired, therapeutic dogs for the aged and the depressed, and police dogs for ferreting out drugs. The dog guards our homes, herds our livestock, and has been known to save our lives. His never-waning devotion assures us he will tolerate our most inane behaviors. A winning combination of confidante and playmate, he's always there to greet us, tongue tumbling out and tail thumping away. This reliable friend deserves the best, and it is obvious why humans have placed the dog on such a pedestal throughout history.

Many celebrities continue in this tradition, and there are similarities between the treatment of today's dog and dogs through the ages. Sylvester Stallone regards his Labrador as a good luck charm, worthy of two first-class seats every time he travels. And when Lyndon Johnson was president, his kennels rivaled France's King Henry's. Although Johnson preferred boisterous beagles to the king's dainty spaniels, he shared the king's enthusiasm for dogs and, like the king, insisted his favorites share his bed.

In 1968 Elizabeth Taylor and Richard Burton thought nothing of paying a small fortune to avoid Britain's six-month quarantine on foreign dogs. They simply rented a yacht and docked it in the Port of London, so they wouldn't have to spend one night parted from their precious Lhasa apsos while

filming a movie in London. Bob Barker echoes the thoughts of many celebrities when he says, "A person who has never owned a dog has missed a wonderful part of life."

Pet owners around the country are showing their appreciation by inundating their beloved pets with canine couturiers, puppy boutiques and designer doggie biscuits, not to mention fire hydrant "toy chests." First Dog Millie Bush even got to write her own memoirs. The phrase "it's a dog's life" has taken on new ramifications, but surely dog's history of working, hunting and fighting for man warrants these slight indulgences. It is unlikely that man could ever find a better companion – any friendship that lasts 14,000 years is worth holding on to.

Past Presidents

F.D.R. with his dog Fala.

There is one position highly coveted among the canine set. If they watch their manners, vote the right ticket and never get airsick aboard Air Force One, they can be prime candidates for the top political pooch position available today – First Dog.

Not to be taken for granted, the First Dog has played a large role in our country's political history. Traphes Bryant, the resident First Dog expert (he was presidential kennel keeper from Truman to Nixon), claims that White House dogs have helped presidents keep a balanced perspective on life and made it easier for the chief executive to win friends for the country, influence heads of state and win elections.

Not all presidents have been this affected by their dogs, but Abraham Lincoln proved his feelings for his four-pawed friend by diving into the icy Wabash River to save his terrier from drowning. Most twentieth century presidents have agreed with Abe that having a dog around is a pretty good thing. Even if a president was not crazy about the species, he had to admit a cuddly puppy could be useful in times of trouble. Both Franklin Roosevelt and Richard Nixon got political mileage out of their dogs.

During his fourth presidential campaign, Roosevelt ran into problems when his opposition accused him of, among other things, sending a United States naval destroyer to the Aleutian Islands (at a hefty cost to taxpayers) simply to retrieve his prized Scottie, Fala. The president proceeded to use the whole incident to his advantage in his famous speech declaring, "Republican leaders have not been content with attacks on me, on my wife, on my sons. No, not content with that, they now include my little dog Fala. Well, of course, I don't resent attacks, and my family doesn't resent attacks, but Fala *does* resent them...He has not been the same dog since...I think I have a right to object to libellous statements about my dog." Fala saved the day, not to mention the campaign.

Inspired by Roosevelt's masterful use of Fala in 1944,

Nixon, under heat for questionable campaign funding in 1952, gave his "Checkers" speech to the largest television audience ever at that time. Fifty-eight million Americans listened as Nixon wryly stated that the one political contribution he would not return was the "little black and white spaniel named Checkers." He continued emotionally, "The kids, all the kids, love the dog."

John F. Kennedy adored his dogs, and his situation is a good example of why the White House employs a full-time kennel keeper. Presidents usually enter the White House with the requisite one dog, but, as people feel compelled to give dogs to presidents, the First Dog soon finds himself demoted to Fifth Dog, if he is allowed to remain at the White House at all. (Incidents such as wetting President Lincoln's bedspread are quite frowned upon.)

The Kennedys came with one simple Welsh terrier, but, as dogs were showered upon them, their menagerie soon included Pushinka, the daughter of Russian space dog Strelka and a present from Premier Khrushchev; Clipper, a German shepherd from the President's father; Shannon, an Irish cocker spaniel from the Prime Minister of Ireland; and Wolf, a wolfhound from an Irish priest with the last name of Kennedy. The plight of most presidents occurs when, as is wont to happen, all the "gifts" have puppies, and the White House becomes more appropriately known as the Dog House. President Kennedy insisted on being greeted by all his dogs every time his helicopter landed, and the family included the entire menagerie on vacations in Hyannisport.

Kennedy's treatment of his dogs couldn't compete with the attention Warren Harding lavished upon his arrogant Airedale, Laddie Boy. This First Dog had his own social calendar and his own special chair for Cabinet meetings. Neighborhood dogs – no doubt Secret Service approved – were invited to Laddie's birthday parties to share in birthday cakes of dog biscuits layered with icing.

No president, though, came close to loving his dogs as much as Lyndon Johnson. When his dog Old Beagle died, Johnson had him cremated and kept the ashes in a box over the refrigerator. Johnson came to the White House with two beagles, Him and Her, and a white collie, Blanco. He was absolutely nuts about the dogs and never left the White House without them. The dogs rode with him in helicopters and limousines and were served from silver trays at parties. He would send out autographed and pawprinted pictures of himself with his pups, and he was the only president known to sleep with his dogs. His favorite came to be a mutt named Yuki (a gift from his daughter Luci), and he said he would "rather sleep with Yuki than anybody." Johnson went so far as to insist Yuki meant more to him than anything in the White House!

President Johnson revealed why presidents have traditionally been attached to their dogs when he claimed that if a president had one friend he could count on he was lucky, and that was why he preferred dogs. Traphes Bryant agrees that "the White House can be such a lonely place that some presidential couples have given most of their affection to their pets." As doggie nanny, Bryant's job required taking the dogs to the presidents anytime they rang.

There has always been a high level of public interest in presidential dogs, and any news concerning the First Dog is a top priority with the press. The First Dog makes the first page with every little bark, such as the front-page headline of an August 1965 *Washington Post*: "Him Found a Her." The whole point of this article was the earth-shattering news that President Johnson's beagle, Him, had been bred.

L.B.J. pats the head of Him, one of his pet beagles, with Freckles, left, and Kim on his lap.

President Gerald Ford with daughter Susan and dog Liberty.

The public interest in the presidents' dogs continued with Rex and Lucky Reagan. Their "press secretary" claims that they received about 10,000 letters a week, mostly from other dogs. She took them to the FBI to be pawprinted so they could exchange pawprints, pictures and birthday cards with their puppy pen pals. When Lucky proved a bit too rowdy (he had a habit of knocking down Nancy Reagan) and was sent back to the ranch, headlines blaring "First Dog Banished" had the country in an uproar. Fortunately his replacement, a Cavalier King Charles spaniel, Rex, was more adaptable to the Reagans' refined White House.

Millie, the Bushes' dog, garnered more press attention than any White House dog ever. The spaniel's memoirs, *Millie's Book*, were on the best-seller list for months, and when Millie was having puppies, the newspapers had a field day with front page headlines such as "Countdown on D-day for Puppies," "First Lady Waits for Puppies," and "George is in the Dog House." After the six pups actually arrived, public sentiment was so high the White House had to compose a thank-you card for all the presents and letters. The card had Millie's pawprint and a print from each puppy as well. During her high-profile stay in the White House, Millie mingled with everyone from King Hussein to Lee Trevino – it was impossible to have an audience with the Bushes without the ubiquitous spaniel.

Although not all presidents are as crazy about dogs as the Bushes, they do have to be seen as dog-lovers – petting dogs is as politically necessary as kissing babies, and this has been true since George Washington's time. In the midst of the Revolutionary War, when General Washington found a dog wearing a collar bearing the name of a British commander, he ordered that the dog be given a good meal and then returned to enemy lines under a flag of truce. Presidents from Washington to Bush may disagree on issues from taxes to defense spending, but one issue they appear to agree on is the appreciation of man's best friend, the dog.

Canines & Companions

Mary Kay Ash

As the door of the pink palace opens, Gigi Ash, sporting pink bows with coordinating toenails, prances out to greet her owner, cosmetics queen Mary Kay Ash. Gigi lives a life filled with all the romance and splendor of Vincente Minnelli's movie.

As the death of her first dog was "like losing a child," Mary Kay relied on Gigi to ease the pain. Ten years later, Gigi has developed into the perfect embodiment of the Mary Kay lifestyle — she wouldn't dream of setting paw outside the house with the slightest chip on her daintily lacquered toenail, and going to the beauty parlor is her favorite activity. Exemplifying her breed's combination of dignity, impudence and vanity, Gigi "knows when she's looking perfect."

Gigi, a finicky eater who "would die before eating dog food," remains svelte without aerobic activity. Her favorite meals are broiled chicken, lobster and homemade cookies, and the poodle is usually able to finagle a special treat out of Mary Kay's son Ben, who often "babysits." She is not adverse to a little flirting now and then and, according to Mary Kay, "Gigi likes men better than women."

This femme fatale is not just another pretty face, and although she has the appearance of an overly teased powder puff, Gigi's pampered exterior belies her shrewd mind. Gigi's absolute devotion to Mary Kay has enabled her to live the life to which she is now accustomed. Maurice Chevalier would have been proud.

Lucille Ball

*L*ucille Ball had always been a dog lover, and, as her first dog was named Tinkerbell because of the way she used to "flit around," subsequent dogs' names all had the word "Tinker" in them. Her last dog, given to her by her beloved husband of many years, Gary Morton, was a white toy poodle named Tinker Toy.

Out of a litter of poodles, Morton immediately knew the one he wanted. "I saw this little dog that was the runt of the litter, and she was the one bossing all the rest of the puppies around. I said, 'That dog I want,'" says Morton. He bought the dog as a surprise for his wife, and the two hit it off immediately.

"This dog never left Lucy's side," says Morton. She would go to work with her and accompany her to the couple's home in Palm Springs. Tinker Toy was a bit of a child prodigy, having been housebroken in three days, and she absolutely adored people. "Her favorite activity was us," says Morton, who still owns seven-year-old Tinker.

"The amazing thing about this dog is that she entertains herself, like a cat. She'll play with one of my golf club covers for hours, and then fall asleep on it," says Morton. "She's also very protective of everybody."

Lucille Ball adored dogs, and once had five at one time, but Tinker Toy always had a special place in her heart. Morton says the two were best friends and even carried on conversations together. Lucy loved her Tinker Toy, and everyone loved Lucy.

Jimmy Barker

*G*allery owner Jimmy Barker subscribes to the "more the merrier" philosophy as far as dogs are concerned. Twenty Cavalier King Charles spaniels currently reside in his Palm Beach and Nantucket homes.

Barker, of Palm Beach's famed James Hunt Barker Gallery on Worth Avenue, adores each one of his pets. The dogs are named Princess, Lady, Empress, Bean, Dillman, Charlemagne, Radley, Rex, Regina, Bows, Buttons, Pig Paw, Poppy Seed, Dandelion, Oliver, Brownie, Winston, Mannie, Marlborough, and King, and Barker says, "I love them all and miss terribly the ones back in Heaven."

Barker became enamored of this elegant breed after his mother left him a collection of Staffordshire figurines depicting red-and-white porcelain dogs. He says, "In 1968 at a London cocktail party in John Singer Sargent's former studio, a lovely blonde Londoner told me of a kennel on Sloan Street that carried the real thing, Cavalier King Charles spaniels." Since acquiring his first two dogs, Duke and Duchess, he has raised over 50, and they all live 15 to 16 fun-filled years.

Barker has many humorous anecdotes to share about his menagerie, including the time he took 23 dogs in a van aboard the Nantucket ferry and lost one. When he returned from getting the dogs water, he found only 22 dogs. He searched everywhere for the missing puppy, Maud, and even grabbed a Boy Scout to search the boat from "stem to stern," and even to look in every car, but they had no success. As the "forlorn" Barker returned to Nantucket in the van, he looked down under the passenger seat and encountered the missing Maud, curled up and sleeping comfortably. "She was absolutely oblivious to the huge stir she had caused," says Barker. "Of course, she got lots of pats and kisses."

It is no wonder that as Barker was leaving his Nantucket photo shoot, he was last seen painstakingly counting his dogs. Staffordshire figurines are easier to keep up with.

David & Jan Bates

As far as artist David Bates is concerned, his springer spaniel, Clovis Lee, has only one fault. "I really miss him not having a tail," admits Bates. "I was wondering if he could have some kind of tail transplant." Until then, Bates comes to terms with this trying situation simply by painting his favorite subject attached to a flowing tail.

Clovis is easily identifiable in most of David's recent artwork – he has been depicted in every medium from oil paintings to brass sculptures and wood carvings. Doing dogs is not new to Bates. "I just like dogs," he says. "I always painted our dog, and when he bit the dust, the neighbors' dogs got done." His house is adorned with wooden sculptures of all his past pets.

David says he chooses dogs as subjects because he can make them look "funny" and they don't care. "You can't do people that way," he says. "Like if you do someone's girlfriend wrong, he'll get really mad. If I was going to do a

commission, it would be easier to do a dog than a person."

Two-year-old Clovis might be easy to paint, but he is a terror around the house. Clovis' favorite activities are chewing on David's paint tubes, watching the paint spurt out, and rolling on bananas in the Bates' bed. "With a dog like Clovis, you have to be a good sport," laughs David's wife, Jan.

One of David's favorite Clovis tales occurred when David was showing his works to a variety of museum curators and a New York dealer. As the prestigious group gathered in the backyard, the sprinklers suddenly burst on, drenching everyone and leaving David speechless. The mystery was solved when a totally soaked Clovis peeked around the corner; he had chosen this opportune moment to find the sprinklers' manual switch. "He does stuff like that all the time," says David.

Clovis has a few other idiosyncrasies. Cheeseburgers are his favorite meal, but he will not eat a bite unless David or

David & Jan Bates
(continued)

Jan sits with him. "He has this whole little eating ritual," says David. "He'll take a bite, play a little, then take another bite...we go through this whole deal every mealtime." The family also sleeps together, with Clovis lying sprawled across Jan and David.

Every morning David and Clovis go to the park, where, after running two miles, Clovis chases ducks and swims. "Clovis loves to swim so much I usually have to go in and get him," says David. Clovis' favorite vacation is the beach, but he never joins his "parents" on their frequent business trips to New York. "He only goes with us if we're going someplace fun," says Jan. "He would hate New York."

Clovis' innocent face and sad eyes belie his rowdy disposition. "He's developed all our bad habits that we don't want to mention," says David. "The only good thing Clovis does is hang around and look cool."

Bijan

Elegance is synonymous with the name Bijan. It is fitting that this handsome designer to the mega-wealthy chooses elegant chows as his pets. The chows, Bearface, Charcoal and Panda, reside at Bijan's lovely Bel Air home, an oasis of green grass and trickling fountains.

Bijan says he chose chows because of their loyalty, but he also enjoys each dog's individuality. Panda, who is named for his striking resemblance to a panda, is known to dance on his hind legs. Charcoal is named for his shiny black fur, and Bearface "looks a little like a bear cub." The dogs also differ in matters of taste. "Bearface likes cheese, and Charcoal and Panda like chicken," says Bijan, "but Panda is on a diet."

These black-tongued, highly independent dogs seem shy around strangers but adore their owner. "I once thought Bearface was trying to show her love by leaving a bone in my bed," says Bijan, "but it was more likely that she was just trying to hide it from the other dogs."

When Bijan travels from his exclusive Rodeo Drive boutique to his other by-appointment-only Fifth Avenue store, the housekeeper takes care of the chows. They love her and let her brush their luxurious coats daily. "These dogs have a nice life," says Bijan's wife, Tracy.

Bill Blass

ill Blass conveys a rare combination of elegance and wit. He is always dapper and polite but never takes himself too seriously. This long-established leader in American fashion wears his elegance comfortably, and, even relaxing at his New England country home, Blass exudes charm. Although the movie star handsome designer radiates style whether wearing a dinner jacket or his country-casual anorak, when his beloved yellow Lab runs and jumps on him with big muddy puppy paws, he does not bat an eye. For all of his urban sophistication, the famed designer is not afraid to get down-and-dirty with his dogs.

Blass has always been an animal lover, and his current dogs – Shelby, a golden retriever, and puppy Barnaby, the yellow Lab – cavort happily through the 22 acres surrounding his stone home that was built in 1770 and served as a tavern frequented by George Washington and Lafayette. Blass, who is famous for his all-American and pretty-yet-wearable fashions, has projected this same simple sophistication in his decor. His home is strikingly neoclassical with gleaming wide-plank wood floors, sleek antiques, and architectural prints, but the house, like his clothing, remains comfortable. No detail has been overlooked, including the towels monogrammed with Shelby's and Barnaby's names, which do come in handy as Shelby is an avid swimmer. "She has a bit of an Esther Williams complex," laughs Blass as Shelby is swimming laps, her body shooting straight up in the air.

Blass is a generous warm-hearted man, and he complains that people are constantly dropping off stray dogs on his property because they know he'll take care of them. He is currently paying for a stray to be boarded until he can find it a home. "People know I'll support anything that has to do with dogs," says Blass. Bill Blass is a true gentleman who enjoys his successes, but realizes quality time is usually time spent in the haven of his exquisitely peaceful country home and time spent alone with his beloved dogs. It is no coincidence that Blass rhymes with class.

Mrs. Alfred Bloomingdale

*I*nternational socialite Betsy Bloomingdale is famous for her chic wardrobe and her great sense of style; therefore, her choice of dog comes as a bit of a surprise. Zozo, named for a Parisian friend, is a huge German shepherd that is neither particularly chic nor particularly stylish but, as they say, love is blind.

Betsy's husband, the late Diners Club founder and chief executive officer Alfred Bloomingdale, shared his wife's love of dogs. He had been so crazy about his daughter's shih tzu that when his son-in-law came and asked for the daughter's hand in marriage, Mr. Bloomingdale said that he would agree to the nuptials only if his daughter would let him keep her dog. The Bloomingdales bought another pet for their daughter and kept their beloved shih tzu for 16 years.

It is not surprising that the Bloomingdales' previous taste in dogs ran from collies to shih tzus. Mrs. Bloomingdale seems better suited to a petite shih tzu than she does to this massive shepherd who literally drags his delicate mistress around her beautifully decorated, orchid-filled Holmby Hills home. She claims she got Zozo and her other German shepherd, Beverly, as protection for the three-acre Mediterranean estate, but her adoration of these two family members is obvious.

Zozo spends her days playing in the abundant gardens and "driving her sister crazy," and the dogs eat special meals that the canine nutritionist brings to the house. This well-mannered woman gets the award for being the most polite to her dog. As she's trying to get the less-than-attentive Zozo posed for her photograph, the soft-spoken Mrs. Bloomingdale repeatedly pleads, "Zozo honey, please sit down" while kissing the dog's nose. Zozo, who is standing up and facing completely in the opposite direction from the camera, does not budge.

President & Mrs. George Bush

She lives in the White House and flies in Air Force One. She is widely admired for her warm personality and down-to-earth manner. She is a great mother and has recently written her own memoirs. Mildred Kerr Bush has it all.

President and Mrs. Bush have always adored dogs, and their last pet, C. Fred, gained fame when Mrs. Bush wrote the book *C. Fred's Story* in his name. Millie, who is named for a good friend of Mrs. Bush in Houston, was given to the Bushes in 1986, and is the most popular First Dog in history. Her story, *Millie's Book*, was on the bestseller list for 29 weeks, and the liver-and-white spotted English springer spaniel's impressive list of admirers includes Margaret Thatcher, Audrey Hepburn, Henry Kissinger, Bjorn Borg and many heads of state. Between impromptu White House gatherings and official functions, Millie's social life is flourishing.

When Millie gave birth to her six puppies in 1989, with Mrs. Bush acting as midwife, they were on the front page of every major newspaper, and Millie was deluged with letters and cards wishing her well. She had her own thank-you cards printed, signed with her pawprint surrounded by six baby pawprints, but all this adulation has not gone to her head. She still remains a gentle, loyal dog who, aside from viewing movies in the ground-floor family theater and sitting in on Oval Office morning briefings, still enjoys life's simple pleasures of chasing squirrels around the White House's 18 acres and, much to the dismay of the White House gardeners, occasionally digging in the flower beds.

When the political climate gets too intense, Millie heads for Kennebunkport, Maine, where the Bushes have been vacationing for 46 years. Millie's not all that crazy about Kennebunkport, where she thinks the Bushes' multitude of grandchildren encroach upon her territory. When they all pile in the Bushes' bed every morning, there is barely enough room for Millie, and, as much as she adores "The Grands," she is not big on sharing her beloved President and Mrs. Bush with anyone. On the other hand, a trip to Camp David is Millie's idea of a good time. She accompanies the president everywhere and presides over horseshoe matches, bowling tournaments, tennis, golf and swimming. There are also hundreds of squirrels everywhere! Camp David is a dog's delight.

Millie Bush shares many traits with Barbara Bush. While they both enjoy living amidst the White House's splendor of gleaming marble floors, massive arrangements of fresh flowers and priceless antiques, they are equally at home digging in their gardens (one digs to plant, the other digs for pleasure). Both Millie and Mrs. Bush appreciate the White House's 94 member household staff but are perfectly capable of taking care of themselves. Both are equally comfortable meeting the King of Jordan or a housewife from Des Moines, and both the First Dog and the First Lady are totally supportive of their best friend, the President of the United States.

Leslie Charleson

Leslie Charleson has starred in the key role of Dr. Monica Quartermaine on "General Hospital" for so long, it is difficult to separate the actress from her TV persona. Like Monica, Leslie is bright, independent and devoted to her career, but instead of being married to the womanizing Alan Quartermaine, she is married to her high school sweetheart, Bill Demms, and while Monica concerns herself with cardiac arrests and international high finance, Leslie's interests lie closer to home.

Leslie has just remodeled her Los Angeles home, and the result is a hilltop retreat as bright and charming as its owner. She spends what little free time she has with animals of all types – she devotes time to protecting dolphins and endangered species, she enjoys riding her beloved horse, and she just adores her cocker spaniel, Freeway.

Freeway, who was a gift from hunky Steve Bond of "General Hospital," was so named because he has a propensity for carsickness, which Steve failed to mention. Unfortunately, in his role as unofficial mascot for "General Hospital," he is forced to endure car trips. "He has had to learn to sleep in the car," says Leslie. "He just swallows a lot."

Leslie is a tiny bundle of energy with a quick wit and robust laugh. She is trying to corral an uninterested Freeway for his photo shoot in nearby Hancock Park, one of Los Angeles' most tranquil areas, but Freeway has other ideas. The spaniel is in ardent pursuit of his favorite hobby, collecting rocks, which is a messy job. Leslie is none too pleased because she has just picked him up from a day at the groomers. She adamantly tells Freeway, "We just paid thirty-two dollars for a fluff and fold and you will NOT roll in the mud!"

Leslie says she has stayed on "General Hospital" for so many years because the Quartermaine family has so much personality. It is surely the wittiest bunch on daytime TV, but maybe it's time for a new addition to the Mansion. What the Quartermaines really need is a dog. Freeway Quartermaine has a nice ring to it.

Dick Clark

ick Clark may have come a long way since his "American Bandstand" days, but his looks haven't changed in thirty years! His busy life must agree with him because today he, as the head of Dick Clark Productions, the "world's oldest teenager," is involved in a breathtaking array of projects.

Upon entering the quaint house that serves as the offices for Dick Clark Productions, one immediately notices the proliferation of dogs roaming around. This charming dwelling is in the middle of Burbank, right across from NBC Studios, but the atmosphere here, although busy, is decidedly homey. It does not look like an office building, and all the offices, which don't really look like offices, remain open. Everyone here seems to be on a first name basis, not just with their co-workers but with each of Mr. Clark's dogs, which happen to be all over the place.

While preparing for the photo, there is a bit of pande- monium as one dog is missing. Mr. Clark's extremely efficient assistant, Carrie, sends out an all-points bulletin

throughout the offices, asking for somebody to please send down Maybelline. It seems that Maybelline just loves to ride on the elevator, and she sits and waits for someone to come push the button so she can get in and cruise around to all the different floors. When she is finally enticed back to the first floor by a promise of going to the beach, Maybelline immediately comes hurling her rather large body down the back staircase and through the hallway, plowing down anyone who might have been blocking her path.

Clark's menagerie includes the robust Maybelline, who "hits everybody's trash at lunch," Molly, a nine-year-old Weimaraner, Alice, a 16-year-old Pekinese/pomeranian blend, and Bernardo, a Labrador/dachshund that Clark found running down the street in San Bernardino. Clark, in his matter-of-fact way, says that he has always loved dogs, and that all of his have been coming to work with him since the "day they were born."

Clark, who currently hosts "TV Bloopers and Blunders" and "Challengers" game show, also produces most television

award shows. Everything from the American Music Awards to the Soap Opera Awards bears his name; he acts as host to Miss USA and Miss Universe and has hosted "New Year's Rocking Eve" for 18 years. He has also recently opened the American Bandstand Grill in Miami, which is filled with his personal memorabilia, and he is planning on opening other restaurants throughout the country. Dick Clark is a busy man, and his dogs seem to know this.

After getting the dogs posed, the photographer takes about four shots, and then Alice, whom Clark refers to as an "oldie but goodie," gets up and starts ambling her way back into the offices. Mr. Clark takes his cue and says, "Well, it looks like the dogs have had enough," and the session is over.

As he enters his huge office that is overflowing with mementos of his lengthy career in show business, he is discussing how different each dog's personality is, and saying how thrilled he was to happen upon poor Bernardo. "Finding him just brought a whole new blush of enthusiasm to the group," he says. No matter how many projects Dick Clark is working on, it is evident that this big-hearted man always has time for his dogs.

Nat King Cole

Nat King Cole with his wife Maria, daughters Carol and Natalie, and their boxer Mr. Pet.

Gary Collins & Mary Ann Mobley

alk show host Gary Collins and his wife, former Miss America Mary Ann Mobley, are two people you cannot help liking. Glamorous Mary Ann waltzes through her front door, kicking off four-inch heels and asking in her perfectly modulated voice, "Would anybody care for a bowl of raisin bran?" It is five o'clock in the afternoon.

True to form, Mary Ann, dressed in figure-hugging silk, does not even flinch as her soaking wet golden Labrador bounds up to greet her. She merely hugs him and asks,

"Don't you just love the smell of wet dog?"

Florence Gene Collins shares her owners' sweet dispositions, but the similarities stop there. Mary Ann and Gary are witty and sharp, but unfortunately Florence isn't the brightest of dogs. Mary Ann says that the Labrador was "not born with a full place setting." She also bemoans Florence's less-than-perfect figure, claiming that, although she's been on Gary's show many times, Florence's next appearance will be when she can "show off her recent weight loss," which has yet to occur. No more five o'clock raisin bran breaks for Florence.

Victor Costa

*D*ress designer Victor Costa has just become a dog lover – D'or Costa has seen to that. D'or, who was named on the day that Victor signed a contract with Christian Dior, is from a famous litter of puppies, and his real name is Wonder Meadow Golden Rod. This is why his name is spelled D'or, meaning "of gold" in French, instead of Dior.

D'or is a Cavalier King Charles spaniel of impressive lineage. His uncle is former First Dog Rex Reagan, and his father is owned by the William F. Buckleys. D'or does not seem at all affected by his famous relatives, although he definitely presides over the Highland Park mansion Victor shares with

Victor Costa
(continued)

interior designer Clay Cope. There are spaniel paintings, spaniel Staffordshire figures, a fireplace screen painted with two spaniels, and books on spaniels throughout the home because Clay has always loved spaniels, and now Victor does too.

D'or is Victor's first dog. "I never had a dog growing up because we were too poor, and then my children were allergic to them. D'or has made a dog lover out of me," he says. "We've bonded." Victor even recently feted D'or with a very social debut party where 52 upper crust canines were treated to a show of doggie fashions from Dallas' exclusive Happy Tails Pet Boutique. Of course, Victor had embellished the outfits with a few designer touches such as Chanel buttons and satin bows.

D'or and Victor are posing for their photograph in Victor's living room. D'or is curled up on his spaniel-sized daybed next to a piano filled with photographs of the multitude of beautiful and famous women that Victor dresses in his sumptuous ball gowns. The designer is suddenly having a few problems handling his new best friend, and looks to Clay for guidance. "Can you make him sleep?" he asks. Then he tries, "Clay, can you make him lie down?" Clay assures him, "Victor, you can do it," and Victor does. The elegant spaniel actually lies down exactly where he is supposed to be. There is a great future ahead for Victor Costa and D'or.

Ed Cox

"I don't know if I'm more devoted to him or he to me," says Texas oilman and art collector extraordinaire Ed Cox, about his black Labrador, Rocket.

This is a rather unexpected admission from the no-nonsense man who lives in the most spectacular estate in Dallas. His Highland Park backyard adjoins the area's most beautiful park, and not many dogs have the famed Turtle Creek as their own private swimming hole. "Rocket's favorite thing is swimming," says Cox. "That's really his first choice – I come second."

Rocket has to confine his swimming to the creek because he is not allowed to swim in Mr. Cox's indoor pool or to play on the indoor tennis court that's lit by an enormous crystal chandelier. Rocket probably does not even appreciate Mr. Cox's incredible art collection. In the mansion's living room alone are enough Monets and van Goghs to fill a small museum, but all Rocket really cares about is that backyard and creek.

Is Rocket a hunting dog? Mr. Cox is adamant that he is not. "No, Rocket is a lover. He is my love," he says, gazing adoringly at the Lab. "Rocket is my best friend."

Mr. & Mrs. Armand Deutsch

A sure sign that people love their dog is when they go to the trouble of writing the dog's biography for their *TOP DOG* interviewers. Harriet and Armand Deutsch of Beverly Hills did just that, wanting to make sure that all the facts concerning their beloved Cavalier King Charles spaniel, Quizzical, were correct.

It is true that Quiz Deutsch has an interesting life. He was born in Lewiston, Maine on the day of the first presidential inauguration of their good friend Ronald Reagan. The couple was in Washington for the occasion and, of course, had no idea that Quiz had arrived on the planet and would very soon become their dog.

Armand and his wife of 40 years, Harriet, had not wanted another dog after their cherished golden Lab, Beau Brummell, passed away. His death was just too painful. However, close friends and dog lovers Frank and Barbara Sinatra had other ideas. Six weeks to the day after he was born, the Sinatras delivered this tiny big-eyed bundle to the Deutsch home, having flown him in their private jet from Maine. They signed the guest book, "Welcome to your new home, Quiz. Aunt Barbara and Uncle Frank." "The first day," said Harriet, "we were afraid that he had left the security of his mother too soon. One day later, we began to wish we had gotten him earlier. He has been a constant joy to everyone in our house."

This elegant couple's home is filled with a fascinating art collection, and Armand, whose family founded Sears, Roebuck, has had many facets to his career. He produced 15 motion pictures for Metro-Goldwyn-Mayer, served as chairman of the family's investment company, and has been on various boards. Most recently, he authored the successful book *Me and Bogie and Other Friends and Acquaintances From a Life in Hollywood and Beyond.* The ever-gracious Deutsches asked the photographer to please take a photograph of Quiz with their housekeeper, Hermenia, whom they admit is Quiz's "best friend." This does not bother either of the Deutsches at all, and they agree that with Quiz, second best is good enough. "We feel like Avis," Harriet says – "we have to try harder."

Quiz's greatest joy is his walks, and the three of them walk together at least five times a week. "He is our trainer and we are his, and it works out perfectly for all three of us," explains Harriet.

The dapper Armand Deutsch, an excellent raconteur, has no trouble explaining their great devotion to their pet. "We feel, as I imagine most other dog owners feel – Quiz's total dependence on us is completely endearing. Also, in a world where complaints seem to be the rule, his quietude is a blessing. We agree with whoever it was who said, 'Let's face it, if dogs could talk, a great deal of the pleasure in owning one would disappear.'" The couple agrees that if Quiz leads what is known as "a dog's life," it is not too shabby.

Senator & Mrs. Robert Dole

MY TOP DOG LEADER
By Senate Republican Leader Bob Dole

My dog's name is Leader. He was a surprise gift from my wife, Elizabeth, who presented me with our Top Dog in the middle of a Capitol Hill press conference the day I was elected to be the new Senate Majority Leader, November 28, 1984 (hence, the name Leader).

Still, W.C. Fields was right: Don't ever try to follow a dog act! Leader got a ton of press coverage that day, including a front-page color photo in *USA Today* – I was simply identified as Elizabeth Dole's husband and the schnauzer's caretaker.

Seriously, Elizabeth deserves a lot of credit for her humanitarian efforts. You see, Leader, now a healthy seven-year-old, was adopted from a Washington, D.C. animal shelter. We are proud of our Top Dog, and we urge all Americans who want to experience the joys of pet ownership to check their local shelters first.

Meanwhile, Elizabeth and I sometimes take turns bringing Leader to work with us. Unfortunately, I discovered the hard way that my office in the U.S. Capitol was not the best place for him – there are simply too many doors, too many opportunities for escape. Leader took advantage of one such opportunity in 1985, shortly after I moved into the historic Majority Leader's office, just a short walk from the Capitol rotunda.

Displaying his own brand of leadership, Leader hot-dogged his way right out the front door. After a frantic search, a call from the Capitol police put us on the trail. Leader was in the rotunda, scattering tourists and yapping with delight. I won't say he resisted arrest, but he did give our officers a real workout.

Since then, Leader has probably had more photo opportunities than most Cabinet members. It hasn't gone to his head, but now he is demanding his own press secretary. I'm not kidding; he has his own press release paper.

As far as tricks go, Leader won't be taking his act on the road, but he does perform one mighty important function. While some dogs bark at the mailman, Leader only barks at liberals.

Michael & Diandra Douglas

Joan Embery

*S*an Diego Zoo queen Joan Embery is nationally known for her animal books and her many appearances on television shows from "Donahue" to "Newhart," but she has really had a chance to showcase both her talents and her rare animals on "The Tonight Show," where she routinely regales Johnny Carson with her collection of rare animals. On the 50-acre Lakeside, California ranch she shares with her husband, Duane Pillsbury, Joan raises all types of horses from miniatures to Clydesdales. She also maintains an assortment of exotic animals, which travel with her on worldwide trips promoting conservation and support for wildlife programs. Her dog, Drifter, might not be exotic enough to appear with Johnny Carson, but she never seems to feel left out.

Joan found Drifter collapsed on her doorstep one night. "She just drifted in one night," says Joan, and now the black retriever is enjoying herself immensely. "Drifter rides all around the ranch on the ranch golf cart, goes to horse shows, and even rides our hitch wagon pulled by two Clydesdales," says Joan.

Drifter has also been known to eat "everything, including bird chow," and doesn't really mind not traveling with Joan, but she is always glad to see her owner return. "Drifter always goes through our suitcases when we return home from trips," says Joan. "She's looking for treats."

Mrs. James Flood

riving through picturesque villages over creaky bridges on redwood-lined lanes, one gradually eases into the world of Mrs. James Flood, whose ancestors were among the first families to settle in San Francisco. The Flood House was one of the only mansions to survive the fire of 1906, and today it houses the fashionable Pacific Union Club. Mrs. Flood currently presides over a 90-acre estate in hilly Woodside, which feels miles away from city life but is actually just a short drive from the heart of San Francisco.

Mrs. Flood answers her door looking quite stunning in her country-chic suede pants and blouse. She is closely followed by Princess Di, her eight-year-old golden Lab, who is all smiles. Mrs. Flood claims Di smiles because she is "thrilled with people," but she's probably equally thrilled with her lifestyle, which includes chasing deer (but never catching them) around her property and lounging in her favorite spot

on the chintz sofa where she has a fabulous view of the serene surroundings.

Like her owner, Di is very well behaved and extremely ladylike. Mrs. Flood says the retriever is a joy to have around, and that this is the first time she has ever had just one dog. She has had as many as six dogs at one time, but Di makes a good companion. Even though her favorite activity happens to be sleeping, Di is always ready for action, says Mrs. Flood. "Every time she sees boots, she immediately wants to go on a walk."

Di enjoys walking around the grounds of her elegantly understated Peninsula home, and she also looks forward to accompanying her owner to the Flood ranch, where Mrs. Flood rides horses and manages her fabulous vineyards, which produce the famous California Sisquoc wine. This elegant matriarch does not sit still for long, and neither does her beloved golden Lab.

Richard Florio & Daniel Kapavik

ichard Florio and Daniel Kapavik cannot walk down the street without being noticed, and from Los Angeles to Paris the bejeweled blonds cause a sensation. These two Dallas hairdressers know how to make an entrance.

"We were at a restaurant in New York, and when Joan Rivers walked in people looked, but when we walked in, everybody put down their forks and knives," says Richard. Of course, after they had been seated, even Joan was a little curious and just had to meet them – within minutes they were all great friends. That's just the way it is with these guys, they don't just dress for high drama – they *are* high drama.

There are two things that every Dallasite knows: if you want to be blond, go to Danny and Richard, and if you want to be glamorous, go to Danny and Richard. Model agency owner Kim Dawson recently affirmed this fact on a "Live

with Jane Pauley" episode featuring the two hairdressers. The two hold court at the exclusive Lou Latimore Hair Salon in Dallas, where they have a large, enthusiastic following and are the leading purveyors of Big Hair in a city known for all-out 'dos.

When not causing sensations or creating glamorous hairstyles, Richard and Danny prefer to spend time with the love of their lives, their 12-year-old ("She doesn't look a day over three," insists Richard) Yorkshire terrier, Baby Jane. "She doesn't know she's a dog," says Richard. "We treat her like a little girl."

This little girl insists on waking Richard up at 5:30 a.m. every morning, and simply will not take "no" for an answer. He then gets up and puts her boneless, skinless chicken breast in the microwave for exactly one and a half minutes and, after she eats this out of a crystal bowl, the two run up and down bustling McKinney Avenue, where Richard and

Richard Florio & Daniel Kapavik

(continued)

Danny live in a glittering highrise. On one of Richard and Baby Jane's morning jaunts, Richard was wearing one of his more avant-garde caftans with his long blond locks trailing down his back. A policeman who was cruising by became so enthralled with this spectacular sight that he actually ran his patrol car off the road and into a neighboring school. There are those who stop traffic, but Richard is in a league all by himself.

Richard is totally undaunted by it all and only wishes Baby Jane would let him sleep. "Daniel says that I must take her to a dog psychiatrist," admits Richard. "He says she's just playing with my mind." Danny also adores Baby Jane, but he leaves the daily routine to Richard. "Daniel does NOT walk the baby," states Richard emphatically.

Danny does accompany Baby Jane when she indulges in her favorite pastimes of going to restaurants and traveling. The four-pound terrier is particularly fond of Paris, where she can actually go inside the restaurants instead of just eating on the patios, and where she can enjoy wearing her little coat with the rhinestone trim. Richard himself is partial to Los Angeles. "I like enjoying life," he says, "and in L.A. there's life."

This dazzling duo could not be more delightful, and they make no pretense of being anything other than themselves. "This is simply how we live and dress," says Richard, and their flamboyant appearance does have its rewards. Whether it's Dallas, New York or Los Angeles, some things remain the same. "We don't ever have to make reservations," says Richard. "There's always a table for us."

Mary Frann

"*I*'m a little worried about this discolored beard, and what about these little tufts of hair?" asks "Newhart's" gorgeous inn hostess Mary Frann. No, she is not discussing her own appearance – she does not have time to care about her own looks. She is totally preoccupied with how her beloved bichon frisé, Panache, will appear in the photographs.

Panache means "vitality and style," and those words perfectly describe Mary Frann. Sitting by the roaring fire in her cozy little jewel of a house in Beverly Hills, the St. Louis native is pretty, sweet and funny, but more importantly she is just nuts about the little dog she recently almost lost through an illness. After much pampering, Panache has recovered and is spending his days playing with his stuffed look-alike dog toy and munching on chicken, vegetables and roast beef. Every two days Mary's housekeeper (and Panache's "best friend"), Carmen, changes his menu "or else he gets tired of it." And Mary says this little fluff ball always sleeps in bed with her because "he's a big snuggler and he

always has to be a part of the action."

Mary has always had dogs, and one day while walking down Melrose Avenue she saw a woman walking a bichon frisé and knew she had to have one. She soon got a puppy, but for the first time ever this animal lover, who works tirelessly for the Amanda Foundation for animals, says she could not think up a name for a new dog. Mary says she didn't want "anything too froufrou," so she had a "name-the-dog dinner party." When that approach didn't work, she had a "name-the-dog contest" at the studio, where she often took the puppy to work with her, and Panache was the chosen name.

Panache seems perfectly happy with his name, but as the photo session draws to a close, Mary still hasn't shown the slightest concern over her own appearance, which does happen to be faultless. She is still worried about Panache. "How is this position? Does he look weird?" she asks. "Oh God, I just love this dog."

Eva Gabor

va Gabor is every bit as colorful as her namesake pink roses. Posing in her Bel Air backyard, surrounded by the vibrant Gabor roses and the beloved Gabor dogs, Miss Gabor is glamour personified.

Mention the roses and you are apt to get a personal tour complete with an opportunity to sniff each fragrant blossom. Mention just one of the four dogs and you will hear a proud mother expounding upon each child's many virtues. Chanting, "Come along darlings," in her lilting Hungarian accent, Miss Gabor sashays through her garden with Lady Ashley, a beagle; Blackie, a black German shepherd, and Miss Magoo and Baby Lion, two dainty Lhasa apsos trailing closely behind.

Miss Gabor believes in treating her pets, including her cat,

Lisa Douglas, as children. She is adamant in stating, "Darling, if you are not going to treat these pets like people, don't have pets. Oh, these children are so spoiled."

The dogs have free rein of the house, sleeping "anywhere they like," which is usually with the loving woman who ostensibly works for Miss Gabor, but actually caters to each dog's every whim. Blackie is the only one that regularly sleeps with Miss Gabor because he's more accustomed to her hours – he prefers sleeping late. The others gather after breakfast in her dressing room as she attends to her makeup.

Eva Gabor is a true dog lover who buries deceased pets in her backyard and who gets teary-eyed at the mere mention of her last dog. She says, "These children cost me a fortune but are worth every penny – they never talk back!"

John Glover

A tiny oasis of Santa Fe style lies in the Los Angeles hills south of Griffith Park. From the turquoise door to the hibiscus-filled courtyard, from the tiled floors to the sparkling pool, this house spells Southwestern charm. Its owner, Broadway and film actor John Glover, appears a little too intense to live in such laid-back surroundings, but his dog Annie seems quite at home.

Annie, so named because she's a "little orphan," was rescued from the pound by animal lover and animal charity supporter John "the day her card was up." John describes Annie's breed as "Basic New York Street Dog," but she actually bears a striking resemblance to Benji. She is wonderful to look at and, aside from being very loved, this "little precious" is smart and talented. She loves to "bark, talk and sing. Peggy Lee and Doris Day are her favorites," says proud Glover.

Talent must abound in the Glover household because John has certainly been blessed with his fair share. The intelligent star of *Gremlins 2: The New Batch* and *Scrooged* is clever and witty with an underlying intensity behind his penetrating gaze. He tends to land parts that take advantage of this intensity, and has been widely acclaimed for the passion he brings to his roles on Broadway and on television, where his work includes a gut-wrenching portrayal of a young man dying of AIDS in *An Early Frost*.

It must provide a much-needed respite from John's fervent career demands to loll away the day lounging around his delightful California home, watching Annie bite at the water sprinklers, but one senses this tranquil scene is not made to last. John Glover may be many things but tranquil is not one of them.

Linda Gray

"Dallas's" Sue Ellen looks great in Armani. Of course, Linda Gray looks great in anything, but as she is partial to Giorgio Armani, she chose to name her beloved German shepherd after the famed fashion designer.

Giorgio was a Christmas gift from Miss Gray's two children, after the death of her previous dog, and he was a bit of a terror from the start. "Before I received Giorgio at Christmas," says Linda, "my son kept him at my sister's house. He was a baby and one day he got caught in her Christmas tree and knocked it down, dragging it all over her house. I'm sure they didn't find it so humorous, but looking back that story always makes me laugh."

That incident was a precursor of things to come. Miss Gray admits Giorgio "flunked dog school," but he does know how to sit, stay and "give you five with his paw." Miss Gray, who, aside from being a versatile and popular actress,

directs and models, has always been a dog lover and has had dogs all her life. She once had a sheep dog, Michael Moo, with whom she had an incredible bond. "Michael Moo and I were definitely friends from a previous lifetime," she says.

Giorgio's day starts by walking with his owner in the mountains by her ranch, and then, after breakfast, he spends his day outside, chasing lizards and playing with Miss Gray's two white kittens. When it's bedtime, after a day filled with "food, sleep and fun," Giorgio jumps right into his special dog bed and falls asleep until the middle of the night, when he is rudely awakened by the kittens. "The kitties push Giorgio out of his bed and he won't complain or anything – he'll just sleep on the floor," says Miss Gray. "The kitties are so tiny and he's so big that it is the cutest thing to see them all playing together. We are all one big happy family."

David Hasselhoff

*D*avid Hasselhoff, famous from TV's "Knight Rider" and "Baywatch," does not have the burly dogs one might expect. As the rugged leather-clad star gathers his dogs, the incongruity of the scene is evident. This heavily-muscled race car driver has chosen to surround himself with six of the tiniest dogs imaginable.

The Hasselhoff family consists of Pomeranians Killer and Jenny; Silky, a terrier; Rusty, a shih tzu; Toto, a Cairn terrier; and Weiner, a dachshund bought because David "always wanted a dog that looked like a weiner." This menagerie also includes four parrots and three cats, all, David says, "because they're cute and I love them." Many of his adoring female fans would gladly change places with any one of these lucky pets, who have free rein of the house, grounds and pool. David admits his dogs lead a good life. "They do have paradise here."

Heloise

"Hints From Heloise" is internationally syndicated in 500 newspapers. Between this column and the 2000 letters she receives every week AND her monthly column in *Good Housekeeping*, the master of this domestic empire, Heloise, still has time for her two adored dogs, Sheeba and Sauvignon. Her devotion to animals comes as no surprise to her millions of readers, and her Saturday column has now become totally pet-related. She says the response has been "tremendous."

Heloise's readers have followed her dogs' exploits ever since her previous schnauzer, Zinfandel, had her rather portly body, and then her new improved schnauzerly-svelte physique published in *Good Housekeeping* in a before-and-after diet photo. Zinfandel developed a small waistline and a large following through these much-heralded appearances.

When Zinfandel died, Heloise was devastated and used her column to assure other pet owners that it is acceptable and expected to deeply mourn the loss of a beloved pet. "I wrote to tell people not to be ashamed of their feelings of great loss," says Heloise. "Pets are not just pets – they are family members. If anyone would say to me that I was being silly because Zinfandel was just a dog, then they don't belong in my life."

She also wrote that it was all right to get another pet after a traumatic loss. "It shows no less respect or love of the previous pet to go out and get another one. There is no way to replace the one that is gone, but I think it's the greatest tribute to that pet to get another little furry friend," she says. "Our life just would not be complete without a miniature schnauzer."

Heloise's current schnauzer, Sauvignon, is three years old and loves romping around Heloise's three-acre San Antonio, Texas home. His favorite playmate is Sheeba, the keeshond Heloise and her husband David adopted a few years ago after she appeared at their barn. The local "Man and Beast" volunteer dog-tracking service could not find her owners, and, after a few months, Heloise realized that Sheeba was here to stay. The "beautiful, beautiful dog" now spends her days watching roadrunners, protecting her owners, and has "turned out to be the sweetest animal," says Heloise.

Heloise's pets do seem to enjoy the limelight. Sauvignon was recently featured in a schnauzer look-alike contest in which he has already received over 600 pictures of photogenic schnauzers, and the photos continue to arrive. Heloise must have the world's largest mailbox.

Earl Holliman

Dogs everywhere should be thankful for Earl Holliman's existence. The "Policewoman" and "T.J. Hooker" star has spent his life making the world a better place for dogs, and as president of Actors and Others for Animals, he has been successful in his mission.

Dogs who have benefited from his generosity include the seven strays that now share his Studio City home, which boasts elaborate kennels, a huge yard and a swimming pool enjoyed by all the dogs. Earl's dedication to dogs is evident by his home's massive gates adorned with dog figurines. The soft-spoken actor has always loved dogs and feels right at home with his current family, which includes Blondie, Puppy, Katie, Maggie, Randy, George and Fanny. The only problem is convincing this excited group to stop chasing squirrels long enough to pose for a picture. Coordinating seven dogs requires great skill; luckily, Earl Holliman is a patient man.

Mr. & Mrs. Roger Horchow

"If you love your dog, you'll do anything for her," says Carolyn Horchow. This expansive attitude is appreciated by Valentine, the black Labrador she and her husband, catalog mogul Roger Horchow, adopted seven years ago.

For this family accustomed to the best, "thousands of calls were made" to procure the perfect Labrador, the breed the Horchows have always preferred for its reliability with children and its good-humored docility. Finally, the right specimen was located and a wiggly puppy arrived on St. Valentine's Day, facilitating the naming process and thrilling the Horchows' three daughters.

Today, Valentine – still wiggling – is the epitome of the carefree canine. Although Labradors are known throughout history for such physical endeavors as braving the icy waters of Newfoundland in search of dropped fish and retrieving shot fowl through the roughest brush, Valentine belies her heritage and chooses to spend her days lounging beside the pool or casually chasing squirrels around the manicured grounds of the Horchows' Dallas estate. When boredom sets in, one bark admits her to the house, where she engages in the more serious pursuit of eating.

Mr. & Mrs. Roger Horchow

(continued)

Valentine will eat anything, and her favorites include Belgian endive (no iceberg lettuce for this family) and pickles. Unfortunately, the bottomless pit doesn't fare as well outside of the kitchen. Valentine has the misfortune of being allergic to grass (a bit of an inconvenience for an outdoorsy type) but, fortunately, periodic visits to the dog allergist have kept the situation under control.

Since Valentine is a "citified" dog, she doesn't accompany the Horchows on their summer sojourns to Nantucket, but Carolyn says the Lab doesn't miss them because of her great baby sitter, "who is crazy about her and loves to spoil her." Sending Valentine to a kennel would be out of the question.

Although Valentine loves people, her best friend is Kittens, the Horchows' "wonderful" cat. According to Carolyn, "They love each other – the cat washes Valentine's face and chews on her ears." Valie never has time for menial tasks; this is one Labrador who does not retrieve. She isn't the brightest of animals, explains Roger, claiming they were never able to train her to do anything, but Carolyn is quick to add, "She's very affectionate. What she is is a companion."

It is fortunate that Valentine thrives on attention, for to be a Horchow is to be accustomed to fame. The Labrador is photographed regularly for publicity and catalog shots, and she has been painted by some great artists, including Roger Winter, whom Horchow commissioned to paint Valentine and Kittens for his wife's birthday. These portraits always accompany the Horchows to Nantucket.

This family adores its dog, choosing to ignore the minor character flaws and enabling her to commit such acts as chewing the bottom three stairs completely away – plaster and all. Carolyn does concede, "I truly believe dogs are more trouble than children."

Marc Jacobs

*S*tuck on the refrigerator of designer Marc Jacobs fabulously eclectic Upper West Side apartment is a fortune cookie fortune that says, "Among the lucky, you are one of the chosen." This could not be more appropriate – the head designer of Perry Ellis was born with incomparable flair, and he uses it comfortably.

With one glance at his unpretentious apartment, much is evident about this handsome and talented young man. Wedged between the elegant pre-war high ceilings and the faded stenciled wood floors and on the casually slipcovered furniture lie random patterns and fabrics, a variety of books, boxes of doughnuts, half-empty packages of Marlboro cigarettes, cassette tapes (from Joni Mitchell to Prince), antique hat boxes and a plethora of dog toys belonging to Jacobs' best friend and sometimes muse, Tiger.

Tiger was the inspiration for a line of Dalmatian print

sweaters shown in a recent Perry Ellis collection – the spots recreated Tiger's light brown and black spots, but the dog has not been much help around the apartment. "I'm not really the type to have a decorator," says Jacobs, whose apartment conveys a true sense of personal style. "Tiger has pretty much destroyed much of what was good, but that's OK. The only thing that really interests me is that the sheets are clean."

The intelligent and inquisitive designer (he reads books with titles like *A Vietnamese Woman's Journey From War to Peace*) had never had a dog before he walked by a pet store two years ago and fell in love with Tiger. Now he can't imagine life without the Dalmatian and hates to be separated from him. "I have to travel a lot," says Jacobs, "but I end up canceling about half of the trips because I don't want to leave Tiger."

John James

"Dynasty's" John James has moved far away from the lavish intrigue of the Carrington clan. He recently bought an 1815 farmhouse on 200 lush acres of upstate New York farmland that borders Vermont. This move allows him to indulge his love of animals, especially dogs.

James, besides being ruggedly handsome, is a truly nice guy, who shares his new laid-back lifestyle with two dogs: Camille, a three-year-old Rhodesian ridgeback, and Cub, a border collie puppy. The dogs traipse happily about the hills, pastures and pre-Revolutionary War barns, and Camille shows very little interest in stopping to be photographed. James says she is a "rather reluctant" star, and, in a way, so is he. James says he will never let his stardom get in the way of the peaceful existence he, his wife and baby daughter have found in the rolling green meadows of upstate New York.

Mrs. Earle Jorgensen

Earle and Marion Jorgensen are very important to the city of Los Angeles. As the founder and Chairman of the Board of Jorgensen Steel, Mr. Jorgensen has long been revered for his business skills and financial acumen, and his wife, Marion, has a sense of style that goes unrivaled. Aside from being very involved with the community, she is widely regarded as one of the best dressed women in the world, and she is renowned for her entertainment skills and her spectacular home. As a matter of fact, former President and Mrs. Reagan have spent every election evening, both gubernatorial and presidential, watching election returns in this fabulous house perched at the top of Bel Air with spectacular views overlooking all of Los Angeles.

The very chic Mrs. Jorgensen, who is a board member of both the Kennedy Center and St. John's Hospital, was

Mrs. Earle Jorgensen

(continued)

recently honored with being the first woman ever elected to the board of the famed Huntington Museum. Mr. Jorgensen, who was a member of Reagan's kitchen cabinet, is still very active in Jorgensen Steel, but this busy couple always makes time for their three German shepherds. Acero (which means "steel" in Spanish), Heidi and Poochie are all very well-behaved and know exactly where to go and where to sit when they come inside the house, its contemporary airy feel conveyed through huge expanses of glass and marble and softened with sumptuous fabrics and antiques. The whole effect is soothing and beautiful, yet it does not detract from the panoramic views shared by the pool and tennis court.

Mrs. Jorgensen expects her dogs to be well trained, but she does this with love. She grew up with German shepherds and is constantly impressed with their intelligence. "These dogs are so smart," she says. "We always have to spell in front of them, and they are still able to understand the basics. Like if I say, 'We are going to go in the C-A-R' or 'Let's get a C-O-O-K-I-E,' one dog goes to the car and the other dog heads right to the cookie jar. It's amazing!"

Mrs. Jorgensen says the dogs can recognize the sounds of certain cars, and even before the gates open they know when family or friends are arriving. The dogs are not trained as guard dogs, but it is evident that they are not comfortable around strangers, and they are very protective of the Jorgensens. When not guarding their beloved owners or their tremendous grounds, the dogs enjoy playing ball with whichever member of the Jorgensens' staff they can coerce into playing with them. Since everybody in the household seems crazy about the dogs, this is not too difficult. "Oh, the dogs play ball all day," says Mrs. Jorgensen. "They keep so busy."

Mr. Jorgensen was unable to attend the photo session because he was called away for a board meeting, but Mrs. Jorgensen insists her husband shares her enthusiasm for the dogs. She says laughingly, "When he's out of town, Earle always says that he never misses anybody but the dogs!"

Harris Katleman

$\mathcal{D}$riving through the gates of the massive Twentieth Century Fox lot is just like in the movies – as one guard is painstakingly critiquing your name and credentials, stretch limos by the dozens continue to glide effortlessly past. When the Wild West suddenly appears on the right and a suburban neighborhood on the left while you are laboriously searching for your specific parking place, you realize that you have truly arrived in Hollywood.

This does not just bear a similarity to the movies – this IS the movies! Behind these doors sitcoms are taping and

features are filming. There are more celebrities within the confines of these gates than there are in a year's worth of *People* magazine, and Harris L. Katleman knows them all.

Katleman is the handsome and powerful president and CEO of Twentieth Century Fox Television. Under Katleman the studio has produced such hits as "M*A*S*H," the long-running "Fall Guy," and currently "The Simpsons," "Doogie Howser, M.D.," and "L.A. Law." This Nebraska native, who has had such an illustrious career, is wild about his two dogs. As Mishka and Trillion are brought into his

Southwestern-style office, which is the size of a small house, this affable man could not be more thrilled to see them. He explains that nothing is too good for his faithful pets.

Trillion, named because she's "better than a trillion dollars," is a golden Lab that Katleman bought in New Jersey and flew to Los Angeles – first class, of course. Mishka (meaning "little bear") was not so fortunate – the Cavalier King Charles spaniel had to fly coach from Oregon. When Trillion recently broke her leg Katleman had only the best doctors on the case. "I didn't care what it cost," says Katleman. "Dogs are the most important thing."

Katleman's adoration for the four-pawed set is renowned – for his last birthday his birthday videotape (what else would you give a studio president?) was highlighted by an interview with his dogs. He bought a jeep just to take the dogs back and forth to his Palm Desert house where the dogs have their own bedroom, and when a "certain actress" he was dating admitted she didn't like dogs, he promptly ended the relationship.

After enthusing endlessly about his dogs' favorite tricks and TV shows, Katleman proves himself a good sport by agreeing to be photographed with his dogs sitting on top of his mammoth desk – seemingly important scripts and papers fly everywhere and Emmys fall over, but he remains unflappable, focusing all his attention on the dogs.

Katleman further endears himself by insisting his guests lunch at the Fox Commissary, at HIS table. What a treat, as his table commands the very center of the huge room filled with directors, actors and producers – a heady experience, to say the least. The waiters wear suits and the 100-selection menu is arranged according to calorie counts. The left side of the page names food categories (everything from "salad" to "junk food"), and the calories progress from crudités to the "Lasorda dog" as the eye travels from left to right.

What a relief to realize that everything's as it should be in movieland. The only unexpected pleasure is Harris L. Katleman himself. Instead of conforming to the cigar-chewing, fast-talking mogul stereotype, he remains a low-keyed and patient man whose heart has been captured, not by resident starlets but by a well-mannered Labrador and a doe-eyed spaniel.

Bill Kirchenbauer

Not many people get a dog and their own television show in the same week, but that is exactly what happened to comedian Bill Kirchenbauer. After playing the offbeat Coach Lubbock in "Growing Pains," the former star of "Fernwood Tonite" soon had his own half-hour comedy series, based on this character. In "Just the Ten of Us," Kirchenbauer stars as a father of seven who accepts a coaching position at a California boys' school. The dog was easier to obtain – he just came from the next door neighbors.

Nielsen was named for television's do-or-die Nielsen Rating System in hopes that the Huskador (one-half Husky, one-half Labrador) would bring luck in the ratings. Nielsen might not necessarily be able to control that, but he can provide affection to Bill and his beautiful and supportive wife, Lynn. Both Kirchenbauers are absolutely crazy about this loving dog, who likes to be "held like a baby" and even has his own toothbrush. Lynn says he comes in and begs for

his toothbrush when they are brushing their teeth. "Nielsen has the cleanest dog teeth in town," adds Kirchenbauer.

The three-year-old's other hobbies include "watching dog TV" and looking out the window of the Kirchenbauers' North Hollywood home. Bill Kirchenbauer's hobbies include cooking and collecting antique radios and jukeboxes, and both Nielsen and Kirchenbauer are very proud of their toys and like to show them off. When Kirchenbauer is not taping his series, he reverts back to his original career of stand-up comedian, performing either on television or in person at major comedy clubs, like The Comedy Store and The Improv, around the country.

Nielsen might not share his owner's talent for making people laugh, but he does have a a bit of the comedian in him. "Nielsen looks a little like Stan Laurel," says Kirchenbauer. "He has that guilty face."

Georgette Klinger

iss Klinger strolls up to the visitors to her Madison Avenue Georgette Klinger Salon and, in an elegant accent, tells one of the group that she is pretty, but does not wash her face correctly. If she is not careful, her pores will be this big (Miss Klinger makes a huge circle with her fingers). As the group is at the salon solely to photograph Miss Klinger with her dog, pore size seems rather irrelevant, but that's just the way Miss Klinger is – one's skin always comes first.

This fascinating woman, who at 75 still goes to her salon every day, is always accompanied by her beloved poodle, Pushka. Miss Klinger is a dedicated public citizen who gives time and money to a wide variety of causes, but she is partial to anything that concerns animals. Pushka goes everywhere with her owner in the Louis Vuitton carrying case that she loves. "The minute I start the day, Pushka knows what's happening," says Miss Klinger, whose ageless beauty truly is the best advertisement for her salon.

Miss Klinger, a Czechoslovakian native, opened her first salon in 1941, and her concept of focusing primarily on individualized skin care has expanded into a multimillion-dollar private corporation, presided over by Miss Klinger, as chairman, and her daughter Kathryn, as president. She currently runs seven posh salons in exclusive areas of Palm Beach, Bal Harbour, Chicago and Dallas. Her New York City and Beverly Hills salons are filled with well-known clients from Helen Gurley Brown to Nancy Kissinger.

Pushka was a gift from Miss Klinger's employees after the death of her adored toy poodle, Pupi, whom she had for 13 years. Now Pushka has full run of the salon and even enjoys the products. She gets a treatment when she leaves a moist climate for one that's dry, and "of course she is bathed in Georgette Klinger shampoo," says her owner.

At the end of the photo shoot, this fabulous woman proves that after 50 years in the business, she still has a one-track mind. Without missing a beat, she puts down Pushka and walks over to the visitor, saying, "Now, about your skin..."

Mr. & Mrs. Tommy Lasorda

riving up to Tommy Lasorda's home makes one realize how unpretentious the beloved Los Angeles Dodgers manager really is. This baseball legend, who could live anywhere, has chosen to remain with his family in the same small Fullerton, California home for over 20 years, and it is overflowing with proof of his friends' and fans' adoration and of his numerous baseball successes. Finding a place to sit becomes difficult because crammed in between hundreds of gifts and baseball trophies lies every Slim Fast diet product ever made. This is a man who believes in what he sells, and, as a walking advertisement for the diet aid, he is trim and fit, with amazingly penetrating blue eyes.

Lasorda is rumored to have an explosive temper with a spirited vocabulary to match, but his tough guy image is totally belied as the baseball legend bursts through his front door, scoops up his miniature schnauzer, Austin, and begs him to "sing for Daddy." Austin gladly complies, and the whole atmosphere becomes rather chaotic. Lasorda is a virtual whirlwind of activity, suddenly making dinner plans (Lasorda's Restaurant, of course), phoning friends, conferring on the marketing of his new Lasorda Spaghetti Sauce, and posing for a picture with his dog.

Austin shares many traits with his energetic owner: he enjoys eating all kinds of pasta, adores sitting in Lasorda's chair and watching what is surely the world's largest television, and is totally devoted to Lasorda's wife of 40 years, Jo. Mrs. Lasorda claims that they have "never in our entire lives been without a dog," and their attachment to their current pet is obvious. Portraits of Austin taken by a special pet photographer hang right alongside artwork painted by the Lasordas' dear friend, Frank Sinatra.

Lasorda counts many Hollywood luminaries among his closest friends, and when the Lasordas lunch at the Twentieth Century Fox Commissary, not one person passes by the table without stopping to pay homage to the man who's been guiding the Dodgers for 42 years. As his friends have always realized, there is an affable side to this dynamic man, evidenced by his love for his family, his devotion to his players, and his gentle behavior with his pets. As Austin is warbling away, Lasorda kisses him and asks with great pride, "Doesn't my baby have a beautiful voice?"

Austin may have many talents, but Frank Sinatra he's not.

Barbara Lazaroff

*B*arbara Lazaroff and Wolfgang Puck are artists. They do not live a conventional life, and no one would expect their dogs to live a conventional life.

Barbara is a designer. Her husband, chef extraordinaire Wolfgang, is the owner of Hollywood's hottest restaurants: Spago, Chinois and Eureka. They live in a home filled with every type of art and animal imaginable. There is a surprise around every corner, including the parrot who's famous for singing "Figaro" with Placido Domingo.

The Puck menagerie also includes a black Lab, Jaguar; Melon, an Irish setter; and a Dalmatian puppy, Zandra (named for Barbara's friend, designer Zandra Rhodes). Barbara is a great mother and even reads *101 Dalmatians* to

baby Zandra every evening, but she says Wolfgang is "like an old-fashioned father. He loves the dogs, but leaves the dirty work to me."

The "children" spend their days "wreaking havoc" in the huge back yard of their West Hollywood home or playing with their pet rabbits. "Oh, the dogs love their rabbits best of all," says Barbara, but their favorite activity is visiting the restaurants. These gourmet canines love the food (lamb bones are their favorite) and relish the attention. The group ends up not getting to bed until 3:30 a.m., but all this socializing never seems to wear thin. Barbara says they love the nightlife; "they're Hollywood dogs."

Liberace

The legendary Liberace is listed in the *Guinness Book of World Records* as the world's highest-paid musician and pianist. "Mr. Showmanship," who was known worldwide for his dazzling jewels and flamboyant costumes, was also famous for his intense, never-waning devotion to animals. This benevolent entertainer spent his life helping animals, his own menagerie of adopted dogs in particular.

Liberace shared his opulent homes with 26 dogs, 9 residing at his Palm Springs hacienda, "Cloisters," and 17 living in his Las Vegas mansion, and most of these pets came to him from people who could no longer keep them. Whether listening to the radio or walking down the street, he was constantly being confronted by tales of people who were moving and couldn't keep their dogs. This soft-hearted dog lover always could be counted on to provide a home for these unwanted dogs.

Liberace's palatial residences became home to an astounding assortment of dogs, pedigreed and mongrel, large and small, and Liberace spoiled them all. Each dog had a sterling silver food bowl, engraved with its name, and special jeweled collars. Jacques, Liberace's smallest and oldest dog, even had ice cream for dessert every night and a special chair that was his alone. Liberace's personal favorites were Jacques and Mischi, another toy poodle, who was with Liberace from puppyhood.

Liberace considered his dogs to be his children, and it gave him enormous pleasure to see that they were all well cared for. This legendary showman took unwanted pets that were in danger of being destroyed and gave them a lifestyle beyond belief, but more importantly he gave them love.

Bob Mackie

*B*ob Mackie represents all the glitz and glamour that Hollywood has to offer. Whether designing for such well-known luminaries as Cher and Carol Burnett or simply for his latest collection, Mackie's designs all share his trademark theatrical flair. Bob Mackie himself is witty, thoughtful, and quite down to earth when talking about his best friends, Pansy and Amber, two aging, yet still glamorous, Lhasa apsos.

Amber, the first dog ever owned by Mackie, was a present from his manager, Phyllis Rabb. "As kids, we were never allowed to have dogs because we lived on a busy street," says Mackie, "and so when I got my first dog, it was a revelation. I suddenly had this great friend who would always love me!"

Mackie soon realized that with his busy travel schedule, between his Los Angeles studio and his showroom in New York, Amber needed a companion. Mackie then bought her half-sister Pansy who was from the same breeder but had a completely different personality. Amber is the more aggressive of the two, but both share a fondness for eating. "Their favorite thing is when I let them lick the bottom of the ice cream bowl and eat what's left – which is never very much," says Mackie.

Amber and Pansy, ensconced in Mackie's home in the hills, lead a life befitting their charismatic owner. "These dogs are typical Beverly Hills dogs," says Mackie. "They go to the hairdresser more than most women I know."

Matthew Margolis

Matthew Margolis gets embarrassed when he is referred to as the "Dog Trainer to the Stars," but he is exactly that and more. Not only is he trainer to the stars, but he has become something of a celebrity himself. One cannot flip through a magazine or switch television channels without glimpsing the elegant owner of The National Institute of Dog Training surrounded by canine companions.

The author of the bestselling *When Good Dogs Do Bad Things* and the mediator of the Beverly Hills Canine Court system claims there is no such thing as a bad dog. "I have never seen a spiteful dog," says movie star handsome Margolis. "It is people who impose these types of thoughts on their dogs."

Matthew Margolis

(continued)

He adores his own dogs, which include a German shepherd, Emily, who can go from aggressive watchdog to cheerful pet with one word from Margolis. He successfully trains many guard dogs that he refers to as "lovable protectors – a burglar alarm with a heart." To watch Margolis work with dogs is impressive - he can make them accomplish amazing feats without ever raising his voice, and it is evident that the dogs are crazy about him.

Margolis believes in training through affection and adamantly states that there is never any excuse to yell at or hit a dog – period. He has one dog that only responds to German; as he shouts out a fierce-sounding guttural command, this German shepherd jumps up on the trainer's chest and starts licking him. When asked what exactly the command was, Margolis grins sheepishly and translates the harsh-sounding words into English as "Love Daddy."

Margolis believes there is no dog that he cannot train, and certainly all his clients, from Doris Day to Cher, can attest to this. This man is truly revered among the dog set in Hollywood for his loving methods of creating obedient pets. Matthew believes there is no joy like owning a properly trained dog. "You cannot live without the proper training. If a dog is not well mannered – who needs it? I want to stop punishment and stop fear."

Why can Matthew Margolis convince dogs to do what nobody else can? He says it is simple. "I just train from the dog's point of view."

Mr. & Mrs. Garry Marshall

*G*arry Marshall has proven himself as a fine director of actors, but no one has passed this along to his dogs. The director of such hits as "Happy Days" and *Pretty Woman* is having a bit of trouble convincing his two cocker spaniels that they don't need to wear their sweaters to sit on a lawn chair on this particular set – the backyard of the Marshalls' San Fernando Valley home.

On this balmy Super Bowl Sunday, Linus, 4, and Lucy, 15, are as restless as their talented owner. Marshall has mentioned that one of the dogs' favorite pastimes is lounging by the pool while he reads, but it is hard to imagine this threesome sitting still for any length of time. Marshall claims the dogs really belong to his wife and three grown children, but his soft spot for them is immediately evident.

Mr. & Mrs. Garry Marshall
(continued)

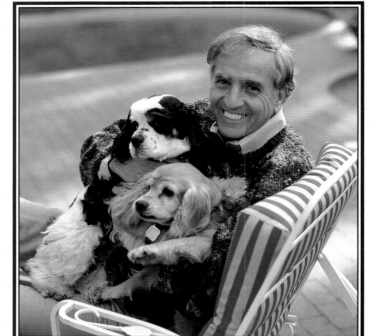

A bit gruff on the outside, Marshall is a teddy bear of a guy whose family always comes first, and dogs have always been considered important members of the Marshall clan. A previous pet, Cindy, given to the Marshalls by Cindy Williams, was always featured in the opening of Marshall's series "Laverne and Shirley." And when Lucy, named for Lucille Ball, went blind in one eye, the Marshalls immediately rushed her to an ophthalmologist and had her fitted with a glass eye.

The newest member of the family, Linus, "from a family of champions, but he's a nobody," divides his time between chasing squirrels and resting in his custom-made bed with its own heater. Both dogs look forward to Saturdays when the entire family gets together for sports games – all those bouncing tennis balls and basketballs! Watching the Super Bowl on TV is not quite as enticing – this is a family that likes to participate rather than observe; yet, as the dogs dutifully follow their owner to watch the football game, another similarity between Marshall and his dogs is evident. All three share a penchant for wearing sweaters.

Mrs. Francis A. Martin

Mrs. Francis A. Martin Jr. is a native San Franciscan whose illustrious ancestors played many important roles in both the civic and cultural development of San Francisco. Her maternal grandfather founded the famed M.H. de Young Museum in Golden State Park, as well as the city's leading newspaper – *The Chronicle*.

Mrs. Martin, a trustee of both the de Young and the Legion of Honor Museums, is a renowned hostess, famous for her beautiful and spirited parties, which usually feature prominent entertainers as well as well-known guests from around the world. This avid follower of sporting events is also an avid gardener who spends a great deal of her time overseeing the magnificent grounds of her estate outside of San Francisco. Mrs. Martin is a devoted lover of animals, and with all of her activities she always finds time for her handsome beige Labrador, Nicol, who is constantly by her side.

Jayne Meadows

honing Steve Allen's and Jayne Meadows' Sherman Oaks home is an interesting experience. If no one happens to be home, the caller is serenaded by barking dogs on an answering machine, leaving no doubt about the importance of dogs in this family's life. Jayne says, "We have a long history of dogs and, although we've had all our dogs on TV, none of them have ever wanted to become stars."

The current Allen pet is Mr. T, a springer spaniel, whom Steve says "does no tricks. In fact, he's not particularly good with such basics as 'sit,' 'stop that,' and 'knock-it-off'." Jayne jumps to Mr. T's defense, saying it's not the dog's fault. She

says, "He's not trained. Because I love him so much, I don't want to be mean."

Steve sums up his feelings on the dog issue with his customary eloquence. He says, "I have given long thought to the mystery of the bond between the human and the canine species. The emotion involved is love, there's no doubt about that, although I'm not sure what purpose it serves in the large evolutionary scheme of things. Perhaps the question ought to be filed under the heading of 'life's mysteries,' a list which tends to grow longer – rather than shorter – as I grow older."

Liza Minnelli

*L*iza Minnelli is a star. The daughter of Judy Garland and Vincente Minnelli has become a world-class entertainer whose concert triumphs, Broadway, television and feature film appearances have earned her Tony, Oscar and Emmy awards. Since she won her first Tony at 19, for *Flora, The Red Menace*, this talented woman has not been out of the limelight, and her beloved Cairn terrier, Lilly, recently made some press of her own.

Lilly got a taste of the pressures of stardom recently when her name and face were plastered all over the tabloids. Liza always travels with Lilly, and when Liza was appearing in Sweden with Frank Sinatra and Sammy Davis, Jr., the dog just went right along. The problem is that Sweden has very strict quarantine laws. Lilly was immediately put under "house arrest" and removed to Paris, where she remained with a friend of her owner until the Swedish leg of the tour was completed; but, in the meantime, the terrier became a worldwide household name.

Lilly was recently more happily ensconced in the 17th-floor suite of the Buffalo, New York hotel where Liza stayed while filming her latest movie, *Stepping Out*. This movie will showcase the star's many talents – singing, dancing, and acting; but all Lilly really cares about is that her fugitive days are over and she has stopped being hounded by the press.

Mary Tyler Moore

"I have loved dogs since I was born," says Mary Tyler Moore. "I had a cocker spaniel who laid under my crib and cried when I cried."

Mary, relaxing with her dogs and horses at her Millbrook, New York Cotswold cottage, has not changed since her "Laura Petrie" and "Mary Richards" days. She is still perky and energetic, but the "real" Mary has a shrewdness and bawdy sense of humor lacking in Dick Van Dyke's television wife and in Ed Asner's mild-mannered news producer. Mary and her husband, cardiologist Robert Levine, are both crazy about animals. "We have a different language we talk to the dogs in," laughs Mary.

Over a fabulous luncheon prepared by her assistant Terry, in the cozy Shaker-influenced kitchen overlooking her lush grounds with seven ponds and waterfalls, Mary expounds upon the virtues of her beloved dogs: Dash, a six-year-old golden retriever, and Dudley, a petit basset griffon Vendeen. "PBGV roughly translates as short-wire-haired-low-to-the-ground-and-the-town-in-France-the-breed-is-from," the actress explains, adding, "I just have the sweetest, loveliest dogs."

The dogs live with Mary in Manhattan and have even appeared on "The David Letterman Show" with her, but they adore their time in the country. Mary says she can't even say the word "country" around them – she has to spell it – and that the dogs know when Friday arrives and it's time to leave the city. "They come with us everywhere we go," says Mary. "The boys are it."

Jack Nicholson

Michael & Marisa Paré

Michael Paré, star of *Eddie and The Cruisers* and *Houston Knights*, has recently adopted a golden retriever puppy, and he's already hooked. Named after Michael's *Streets of Fire* character, Tom Cody, the puppy Cody has already licked his way into this striking actor's heart and accompanies his owner everywhere, including his movie sets.

This type of relationship is nothing new to Michael, who claims that as a boy he was "closer to his pet Rottweiler than anybody else." Laid-back Michael is happy with his choice of pet. He says, "It's good to have a dog that likes to hang out."

Mrs. Allen Paulson

*I*t is not surprising that Madelaine Paulson's dogs have probably logged more air miles than most people. Since her husband, Allen Paulson, is CEO of Gulfstream Aerospace Corporation, the dogs get ample opportunity to fly, and on the morning of her photo shoot Mrs. Paulson and her three cherished canines – Frosty, Lido,

and Dobie – had just helicoptered into Los Angeles from Palm Springs.

Frosty, a well-groomed standard poodle, Lido, a Chihuahua with a rhinestone collar, and Dobie, a miniature Doberman, have full run of Mapleton House, the Holmby Hills mansion originally built in 1938 by famed architect

Mrs. Allen Paulson

(continued)

Wallace Neff. "I just would not be without a dog," says Madelaine, who gave Frosty to her husband as a wedding present two and one-half years ago. Now Allen is as crazy about the animals as his wife and even keeps Frosty's brother at their Savannah home so as not to spend even one night dogless.

Madelaine claims the dogs spend their days "eating, sleeping and getting their tummys rubbed," but in reality they have a full-time occupation trying to keep up with their glamorous owner in this massive estate, which used to be owned by Joan Bennett and was recently featured in a five-page spread in *Town and Country* magazine. Madelaine is a whirlwind of activity whether she's staging numerous charity benefits, preparing for the Kentucky Derby (where one of the Paulson horses is running), or planning Lee Iacocca's nuptials, which took place at her home. Incidentally, Lido, Iacocca's namesake, wore a doggie dinner jacket in the wedding.

In spite of this fast-paced lifestyle, dogs are a top priority with the Paulsons. Madelaine, who has always been an animal lover and says she would just fill her home with dogs if her husband would allow it, is already scheming to acquire another standard poodle. She is holding a Canine Angels Golf Tournament in Palm Springs benefiting three of her favorite charities, Canine Companions for Independence, Guide Dogs for the Blind, and Guide Dogs for the Desert, making sure the dogs attend both the celebrity-filled tournament and the following dinner, at which there will be an auction. Not strictly coincidentally, one of the items to be auctioned happens to be a standard poodle. There is a good chance that Madelaine Paulson will be flying back to Los Angeles with three dogs PLUS a new addition to the Paulson home in tow.

Michelle Pfeiffer

Mr. & Mrs. T. Boone Pickens

T. Boone Pickens might run Mesa Petroleum, but his two-year-old papillon, Sir Winston, definitely is CEO of the Pickens' Highland Park mansion, recently purchased when the oil king moved his family from Amarillo to Dallas. The house is filled with an array of Winnie-oriented artwork and furniture, including a fireplace screen in his likeness, painted by the Pickens' daughter. Actually, last Christmas all presents were related to Winston in one way or another.

"Winston likes to think of himself as an only child," explains Pickens' wife, Bea, and although the dog-loving family has 32 pointers and 6 Labradors at their Amarillo ranch, Winston has to share his Dallas home with only a green parrot named Wall Street. Winston travels "all over the country" on the Pickens' private plane and sleeps with them in bed. Like his owner, whose name has recently dominated the news with his attempts to gain a board seat on a Japanese company and with his ongoing crusade to improve shareholders' rights, Winston is not averse to a little publicity, and actually smiles when posing for photographs. Winston is more human than dog in most respects.

Even his food preferences don't include traditional doggie favorites. "Winston eats anything Bea eats," says Pickens. These days he happens to be on a popcorn kick and it's all he ever wants to eat. Not plain, of course, but caramel.

President & Mrs. Ronald Reagan

One dog's misfortune is another dog's gain. At least that is the case with Rex, the Reagans' seven-year-old Cavalier King Charles spaniel. After their first dog, Lucky, got bad press for dragging around the delicate First Lady and being altogether too boisterous for the White House, he was relocated to the Reagans' Santa Barbara ranch. Lucky didn't seem too concerned and was actually quite happy at the ranch, but his removal allowed Rex to slip right into the coveted First Dog position.

The chestnut-and-white spaniel was named after a valued member of the Reagan White House staff and had many special privileges as First Dog. He enjoyed his frequent helicopter forays and just about every other aspect of White House life. Aside from his daily walks and play periods on the South Grounds of the Rose Garden, Rex spent most of his time in the private quarters with Mrs. Reagan.

Rex appreciated his four fun-filled years at 1600 Pennsylvania Avenue, but he seems to be adjusting well to "normal" life in Bel Air. His home on St. Cloud Road has one and one-quarter acres of land for him to play on, and he enjoys having such glamorous neighbors as Zsa Zsa Gabor and Elizabeth Taylor, who live down the street. He does not seem too upset about having to relinquish his title as First Dog to Millie Bush...possibly because nobody has ever told him.

Dan & Pam Reeves

an Reeves, who is in his tenth season as head coach of the Denver Broncos, has played in or coached eight Super Bowls. He is one of the youngest and winningest coaches in the history of the National Football League, but he always makes time for his family, which includes wife Pam, three children, Dana, Laura, and Lee, and two adored golden retrievers, Jake and Hondo.

Hondo, who was named for the town in Texas near the Reeves ranch, is three years old; and Jake, named after a movie character played by John Wayne, is eight. Both dogs are playful and have a penchant for scrambled eggs. Jake's biggest trick is "saving" the kids when they "play dead" in the pool, but, strangely enough, neither dog has shown any interest in catching the football.

Joan Rivers

$\mathcal{S}$pike Rivers Rosenburg is his real name, but he's known professionally as simply Spike, "the way Cher is just Cher." This four-year-old Yorkie, whose weight barely exceeds his age, has become something of a national celebrity. Slides picturing his slightly scraggly little body have been flashed repeatedly on "The Tonight Show" and "The Late Show," and his fame increases with each personal appearance in the arms of his "mother," comedienne Joan Rivers.

Spike was given to Joan by her daughter's former governess, who said Joan was going to need somebody to love when her daughter left for college, and Spike has since made quite a name for himself. Joan refers to him constantly and he accompanies her everywhere from Las Vegas to Rome.

Joan Rivers

(continued)

"He was brought up on airplanes," says Joan, and he even flew on Air Force One with First Dog Lucky Reagan. Joan concedes that "Spike has led a very interesting life."

With his meteoric rise to fame, it's not surprising that, in Spike's rare moments at home, he is king of the castle. "Spike rules the roost, and with four sisters that's no small feat," says Joan. Especially when the sisters happen to be German shepherds.

As Spike was Joan's first male dog, she felt he needed a "macho" name. The Yorkie also proves that manly can still mean finicky. "Spike is the only dog in the world that does not eat," says Joan.

Joan, who has always loved dogs and can never remember being without them, is a big supporter of animal charities, including Guide Dogs for the Blind, where a number of the dogs have been named in honor of her late husband, Edgar.

Since he is a "wonderful traveler who doesn't make a peep," it is easy for Spike to keep up with Joan's busy schedule. Wherever she's appearing, Spike is always there to come out on stage for the final bow. Joan says he wouldn't miss it. "Show biz is his life."

Carolyne Roehm

As Carolyne Roehm answers the door of her Sharon, Connecticut estate, she is an unexpected pleasure. Yes, she is as tall and graceful as she appears in magazines, and yes, she is the very vision of country chic, but that's a small part of Carolyne Roehm. This beautiful soft-spoken woman is talented, gracious, and has a great sense of humor. She takes her magnificent surroundings in stride.

Carolyne and her husband, RJR Nabisco king Henry Kravis, spend most of the week in their New York apartment, but both live for the time they can spend at their 60-acre estate with their horses and their dogs. It says a lot about Carolyne that her stables are more extravagant than her comfortably elegant nineteenth century home. She has spared no expense on keeping her horses in style, and from the indoor arena with the spectacular sound system (Carolyne is "mad" about music) to the roomy stalls with the gleaming brass nameplates, these stables, which took three years to build, are outstanding.

Carolyne adores all animals, especially her dogs, Nabisco, Christy, and Pookie. Pookie, the West Highland white terrier who accompanies her everywhere, is somewhat of a celebrity himself because of his appearances with his elegant owner in ads for the simple, classical and expensive clothing that she designs (she truly is her own best model). Her husband, Henry, shares her devotion to the dogs. "We're both a little whacked out about our dogs, I must admit," says Carolyne.

This avid gardener and rider says, "I don't know anyone who doesn't love his dog. I'd rather talk about my dogs than anything." Pookie is pleased about that, but what makes him happiest is food. "Food is definitely the way to Pookie's heart," says Carolyne. "I'd like to say he's totally devoted to me, but the truth is, he's devoted to whoever feeds him." Fortunately, with Nabisco owning Milk Bone, these dogs never have to worry about running out of dog biscuits.

Jack Scalia

What type of person would have not one, but two, powerful Rottweilers? If "Dallas" star Jack Scalia is any indication, this person would be serious, strong and well-disciplined, with a hint of hidden aggression.

Unfortunately, Jack's two pets, Nitro (with the 20-inch neck) and Tara (with the pink bow) are not as adept at hiding their aggressive tendencies. In his direct manner Jack insists that to him the dogs are nothing more than "lovable pets" who only strike when met with aggression, and the three do have an amazing bond; the Rottweilers have twice saved Jack from attackers.

The handsome marathon runner insists that his wife, a former Miss World, also loves the dogs, but he admits that she really had no choice. "I was not going to get rid of the dogs," he states. Jack does claim that having the dogs helped prepare him for the recent arrival of his new baby. "Nitro and Tara are so childlike," he says. "They have taught me a sense of responsibility and patience."

The conversation is suddenly interrupted by the arrival of 120-pound Tara, who wants to have her ball thrown repeatedly. One dares not disagree. Hopefully, in a few hours she'll move on, either to another pastime or another victim.

Dina Schmidt

arisian dogs eat out all the time – no self-respecting French restaurant would dare turn a chic *chien* away at the door. Unfortunately for New York dogs, canine liberation has yet to hit the streets of America. Dina Schmidt's Upper East Side restaurant provides the next best alternative. If you can't take your dog inside a restaurant, at least you can get a table beside his photograph.

The walls of the Summerhouse Restaurant and Bar are filled with photographs of dogs whose owners have responded to the sign on the door saying, "Summerhouse Needs Pictures of a Few Good Dogs." Now the walls of this wittily elegant restaurant are covered with a wide variety of canines, and the clientele has expanded from the "ladies who lunch" group. "All people love to come in and sit by their dogs," says Schmidt, who also owns Juanita's, a hip Tex-Mex eatery in the neighborhood.

In the evenings the Summerhouse bar really hops – it has a "Cheers-type" ambience and the food varies between stylishly nouvelle and shamelessly hearty. Schmidt's Great Dane, Beau, causes a bit of a stir when he enters the restaurant for his photo shoot, but he does not seem to realize that he is canine. After all, he has taken a taxi to the restaurant. "Beau loves to ride in cabs, especially when it's raining. He just hates the rain," says Dina's daughter, who helps in the restaurant.

Dina Schmidt

(continued)

This Madison Avenue restaurant is filled with many dog-related items besides the photographs. The front window displays a table set up with two stuffed dogs enjoying a meal; the restaurant sign is decorated with festive lights shaped like Dalmatians and fire hydrants; there is a sign for "Doggie Take Out"; and there is a big bowl of dog treats by the door. The dog treats are labeled so as to prevent customers from confusing them with people treats, although inevitably overzealous eaters fail to read the sign on the bowl, saying:

Here's a Treat
For one to Eat
Yet there's a Catch
You must have 4 Feet.

Parisian restaurants might serve dogs meals, but Summerhouse gets the award for after-dinner snacks.

Marge Schott

*S*chottzie Schott is a familiar figure to baseball fans. This robust St. Bernard goes everywhere with her owner, Mrs. Marge Schott, owner and CEO of the famed Cincinnati Reds, and is universally adored. "Schottzie gets more fan mail than I do," says Mrs. Schott, "and always better gifts."

Schottzie, whose name (slightly modified) means "sweetheart" in German, likes to answer her own fan mail, of which she receives "a ton." She has corresponded with Millie Bush and Lucky Reagan, and the mail is always filled with pictures of interested "suitors." When she is not answering her legions of mail, this media darling's hobbies include "sleeping, snoring (loudly) and making public appearances," says Mrs. Schott.

This unofficial mascot of the Reds loves to appear in front of her fans, and one day while Mrs. Schott was in her office waiting to go down to the field, Schottzie, donning her Reds baseball cap, casually strolled down the hall to the elevator on her own. "We had a new elevator operator that day," Mrs. Schott recalls, "and he nearly flipped when he arrived at the third floor, opened the door, and Schottzie just stepped right on in for her ride to the field. She does love elevators."

Mrs. Schott grew up with dogs, and when she was given a St. Bernard by an old boyfriend, she fell in love with the breed. This hard-working woman, who also owns several large Cincinnati automobile dealerships, contributes to many animal charities, including Pets Helping People and the Animal Rescue Fund, and adores all animals. Schottzie is lucky to have such a festive owner who lets her indulge in all her favorite pastimes, including eating, which is of prime concern to the 170-pound St. Bernard. What are her favorite foods? "Schottzie eats anything and everything...but especially my dinner!" says Mrs. Schott.

Bobby Short

obby Short in his stylishly simple Sutton Place apartment is a different man from the Bobby Short who sings his heart out every night at Cafe Carlyle. When not performing, he is more relaxed and his every word and movement connotes elegance. He is at ease among his eclectic collection of furnishings and artifacts, ranging from Le Corbusier chairs to Nigerian bronze heads to wild splashes of contemporary art, and has an extensive collection of African tribal art. His many bookshelves are bursting with the books this voracious reader devours when he's not working, and his home is filled with the boisterous presence of his Dalmatian, Chili.

On a rainy day by the fire in his loft-like living room, Short is recounting the time that Chili, an avowed "chocoholic," stole a piece of chocolate from a house guest's pocket. The jacket was hanging in the closet and Chili went in and ripped out the entire pocket that containing the chocolate, and proceeded to inhale the whole thing on one

of Short's white sofas. "Chili always steals food," says Short. "In France, he eats all of his dinner and then eats the cat's too."

Short always takes Chili when he vacations at his home in the South of France. There Chili is able to accompany his eloquent owner to restaurants and swim in the pool that Short has equipped with special steps for his beloved Dalmatian's swimming convenience. Chili has a good life and adores people and attention. "I think he even enjoys being photographed," says Short. "You know he is so vain."

Chili, who was named after movie star Chili Williams (who only wore polka dots), and Short have become the best of friends. They do everything from exercising to cooking together, but there is one major difference between the Dalmatian and his legendary owner, who's been holding court at the Carlyle for 24 years. "Chili just couldn't care less about music," says Short.

Richard Simmons

Gone With The Wind is being remade. The stars, Ashley, Melanie, Scarlett, Prissy, and Pitty Pat, will be accompanied by newcomer Marty, but in this version all six leading characters happen to be dogs, Dalmatians to be exact.

The setting is fitness guru Richard Simmons' white colonial house, the "Tara" of Beverly Hills, and the stars are busy rehearsing the birthday party scene (with Richard directing, of course). Things have not been going well since Ashley sneaked out and ate the top layer off the color-coordinated birthday cake.

Ashley, who is not fond of the other dogs, is causing many problems. Dalmatians are notorious for holding grudges and, since Richard claims "Ashley likes to pretend she's the only dog," the other five sit and snarl at their errant sister, who is now suffering from a mild case of sugar shock.

Richard says he chose Dalmatians because they are the most "whimsical" breed. He keeps the girls in shape through rigorous morning workouts and steers them away from junk food.

Whenever Richard is in town, he takes the dogs to his TV locations. When he's away, the dogs stay with Elijah, Richard's good-natured manager, and Edna, his housekeeper, who "takes all six dogs cruising down Sunset Boulevard in

Richard Simmons

(continued)

the Mercedes convertible." Richard is a testimony to his profession; his refrigerator is filled with Richard Simmons Diet Products and his staff members have lost a total of at least 100 pounds.

Richard's house, which coincidentally was recently used for stills of another version of *Gone With The Wind* (this one featuring people), revolves around the Dalmatians. Not only does everyone cater to the real Dalmatians, but there is Dalmatian-related paraphernalia strategically placed throughout this spectacular home. Even the mailbox has been painstakingly painted with one hundred and one of the spotted creatures.

Meanwhile...back to the birthday party. A new cake has been delivered, and everyone is in place. As the photographer is yelling at Prissy to get back in her chair, Richard informs him that poor Prissy is deaf. Not to fear – Elijah adds that she does read lips.

It does not appear that this version of the classic will be released in the near future. Perhaps this troupe would be better qualified for a remake of *101 Dalmatians*.

Marina Sirtis

arina Sirtis has just received a new puppy so small that if you don't look closely you'll miss him. This minuscule Yorkshire terrier was a Valentine's Day present from Marina's musician boyfriend. "I had wanted a Yorkie all my life," says the striking raven-haired star of "Star Trek: The Next Generation," "but this was a total surprise. I thought I was getting a car stereo."

The half-Greek native of London chose an appropriate name for her new puppy – she named him Skilaki, which means "little dog" in Greek. This particular little dog gets positively lost in Marina's new home, which is literally perched on a North Hollywood hillside. The decor is understated and contemporary so as not to compete with the spectacular view from the huge windows and from the heights of the terrace. It is the perfect setting for this quick-witted beauty who plays "little Miss Perfection," Deanna

Troy, in the Emmy-winning drama. She is the Mr. Spock (half-human/half-betazoid) character of the nineties, albeit a little prettier to look at. "Spock had the funny ears and I have the funny eyes," says Marina. Her incredible eyes have a mysterious translucence to them, making her very believable in her role as the Starship *Enterprise's* resident psychologist, who has the extraordinary ability to read people's emotions.

Skilaki is Marina's first dog, and she's having a little trouble housebreaking him, but she's sure the confusion will wear off. She has had cats all her life and her two cats don't quite know what to think of this diminutive creature that chases them around, but the household is gradually adjusting, and Marina is thrilled with her puppy. "I didn't know I was a dog person until I got Skilaki," she says.

Liz Smith

America's most powerful gossip columnist, Liz Smith, has a high energy level that is shared by her two beloved dachshunds, Calypso and Odysseus. Their average day, according to Liz, involves "waking, jumping off the bed, running, barking, eating two meals, sleeping, walking, napping, playing ball, greeting, barking, being pests, and sleeping."

The abundance of napping in this schedule must stem from exhaustion. The dogs have to work hard to keep up with their indefatigable Texas-born owner, whose columns are syndicated in 60 newspapers and whose commentaries air on 129 television stations. Liz chose the dogs for their "sweetness" as well as their energy level, and named them for characters in the *Odyssey*. "I decided on a Greek motif," she says, "and Calypso and Odysseus were lovers."

The canine Calypso and Odysseus choose to amuse themselves by searching for the odd crumb, and they recently both got their heads caught in the same empty biscuit box. Nine-month-old Odysseus also has a special penchant for chewing on "anything – from camera straps to shoes to underwear." There is never a dull moment around Liz Smith's Manhattan apartment.

Candy Spelling

What do you do when your dog will drink only Evian? When she turns up her delicate nose at the mere presence of tap water? If you're the Aaron Spellings, you indulge her. And this bichon frisé has never fallen for the put-the-tap-water-in-the-Evian-bottle trick; she demands the real thing!

Although the dog in question, Shelley, doesn't "rub noses with the rest of the dogs and likes people toys better than dog toys," producer Aaron Spelling and his wife Candy do have three other dogs in their 58,000-square-foot Holmby Hills mansion that has its own bowling alley. The canine members of the Spelling family include Pepper, "a very insecure New Zealand terrier" given to the Spellings by Ricardo Montalban after the dog's short career on "Fantasy Island"; Angel, a poodle who continues to bite the mailman on a daily basis; and Muffin, "the nervous one" who's a vegetarian and would "die before eating meat." "It has gotten to the point that she will now only eat vegetable Milk Bones," says sweet and glamorous Candy.

Add Shelley, who insists on upsetting the others by blocking the doggie door, and the only peace and quiet around this palatial Beverly Hills home is when the dogs are off on their Friday trek to the beauty parlor (this particular groomer did require three references before she would even consider taking the dogs). You won't hear any complaints from the Spellings, though, because they absolutely adore their pets and travel by motor home so they can take them along on their journeys. Aaron never wants to be away from his beloved dogs.

The Spellings have always been crazy about animals, and last Christmas, Candy had four little china Battersea boxes made in England for their daughter, Tory, each containing the portrait of a Spelling dog. According to Candy, "There is not an animal charity we don't support," and the four Spelling dogs can surely attest to that. Charity begins at home around the Spelling household.

Roger Staubach

*I*n the history of football, there has been only one player to win both the Heisman Trophy and the award for Super Bowl Most Valuable Player, and that was legendary Dallas Cowboy quarterback Roger Staubach. After his stellar career as Number 12 on "America's Team," where as starting quarterback he led the team to four Super Bowls, Staubach then settled in Dallas with his wife, Marianne, and five kids. He is now the head of his own immensely successful real estate agency, The Staubach Company.

Roger is regarded as an all-around good guy in Dallas. He is known to be deeply spiritual, and there is not anyone with a bad word to say about this rugged family man. The Dallas quarterbacks, past and present, have always remained close,

and on the day of his photo session Roger has invited the current Cowboy quarterback, Troy Aikman, to dinner at his North Dallas home.

Roger and his 14-year-old daughter, Amy, are posing with their beagle, Sky, who was named for Sky Ranch, the Cowboys' headquarters where the dog was found. Even though Sky is the family dog, he's partial to Amy and sleeps with her in her bed – under the covers.

While trying to get Sky to pose, mild-mannered Staubach quips, "Tell Sky a joke. He likes jokes." It is plain to see that Staubach, in his own noncommittal way, is a true dog lover. When asked if he adores dogs, his reply is characteristically understated. "They're O.K.," he says.

Mr. & Mrs. Jimmy Stewart

Jimmy Stewart is a national treasure, but his dog, like his home, his elegant wife, Gloria, and himself, is totally unpretentious. Barron Stewart was a stray golden retriever who had the good fortune to stumble upon the Stewarts about five years ago. "We were out of dogs," says Stewart, a well-known dog lover who brought Johnny Carson's audience to tears when he was a guest on the show. The 82-year-old star had read one of the sentimental poems he has written about his previously owned beloved dogs.

Barron's timing was right, and he now finds himself cavorting through the Stewarts' Beverly Hills grounds, mingling with Hollywood royalty, and enjoying meals from

Mr. & Mrs. Jimmy Stewart
(continued)

the Stewarts' chef, whom many claim is the best in town. Barron eats whatever the Stewarts eat, along with the special dog cookies the chef whips up especially for him. "What Barron eats depends on the day," says Mrs. Stewart. "What we give him for lunch, we could have for dinner. He likes beef stroganoff." The dog also has access to the next-door lot that Mr. Stewart bought as a surprise for his wife, whose passion is gardening. The huge corner lot actually serves dual purposes – it houses Mrs. Stewart's bountiful garden as well as providing an exercise area for the Stewart dogs. A large sparkling pool engulfed by fragrant blossoms occupies the original back garden.

This lifestyle all sounds more glamorous than it really is.

Jimmy and Gloria Stewart are two of the most down-to-earth people in Los Angeles. This is a man who actually waves to the deluge of tour buses that pass by his house at all hours of the day, and Mrs. Stewart periodically interrupts her conversation to matter-of-factly dash out to place a red flag where Barron leaves a deposit in the yard so the gardener can find it. Throughout their 43 years of married life, this animal-loving couple has never been without a pet, and the dogs that have been fortunate enough to live with the Stewarts have probably never given a second thought to their surroundings. All the animals realize is that their owners are something special. Barron will probably never know how lucky he is.

Martha Stewart

*B*reakfast with Martha Stewart is a soothing experience. In the converted barn that serves as America's favorite hostess' spacious kitchen, on a rainy day at her nineteenth century Westport, Connecticut farmhouse, all is as it should be. The kitchen looks exactly as it does in the luscious books, videos and magazines scripted by this queen of good living; her gardens are abundant with spring tulips, and even her chickens appear fluffy and good-natured. The only incongruity in this picture is Martha Stewart herself. Instead of the prim housewife who appears on her book covers, this former model is sleek and sexy with a wicked wit, and her talent and perfectionism are evident everywhere.

Contributing to this picturesque scene are Martha's perfect (what would you expect?) pets, her three

Himalayan cats and two chows, Max and Zuzu. Between her cooking seminars, TV appearances, books, videos, and magazines on everything from entertaining to weddings to gardening, Martha always finds time for her beloved pets. Both dogs travel with her when her schedule is not too demanding, and always accompany her to her house in the Hamptons. "The dogs love to go on planes," she says. "They run through the airport and hop in their seats to look out the window. They know exactly where they're going."

Max, who is eight, is named after the Beatles character, and Zuzu, who is eleven, is named after Zuleika Dobson, the novel character who was the most beautiful girl in the world. "My Zuzu *is* the most beautiful girl in the world," coos Martha. On her rainy-day photo shoot, Martha is every bit

the professional. She does not want the umbrella to shield her from the rain during the breaks between shots – she wants it covering the dogs. She is more concerned about the chows' hairdos and their poses than she is about her own. "I just don't want Zuzu to look stupid," she says.

The dogs have a happy life, running around the beautiful grounds hunting woodchucks and chasing deer. "Of course they never hurt anything," says animal lover Martha. As breakfast progresses in the cozy kitchen, Martha asks her assistant for some "homey" jam. As successful, worldly and talented as Martha Stewart is, the key to her success is that she, sitting at her massive oak table, munching on freshly baked croissants with her dogs lounging at her feet, remains "homey."

Sally Struthers

*S*ally Struthers loves animals and children. This is evident in her cozy Beverly Hills home filled with children's artwork, a huge collection of ceramic animals, and a multitude of living animals, including three chows and one large, unidentifiable ball of fur.

Chester, Sally's first chow, is the most gregarious. His favorite activities are tearing the wrapping paper off gifts and posing for pictures. Chuckie and Eddie, the twins, are very shy, and Hailey, a 150-pound Newfoundland, sticks close to his "favorite playmate," Sally's 12-year-old daughter, Samantha.

Sally, who grew up with cocker spaniels, had never seen a chow until she discovered a whimsical Icart painting of a blonde lady with a red chow. She immediately had to have this breed of dog, and soon ended up with three "Don King look-alikes" who, along with Hailey, somehow all manage to wedge themselves into Sally's bed every night.

Samantha claims that Sally "commits her life to the dogs," and it is true that Sally is a very dedicated woman, whether giving to her numerous philanthropic causes, to her daughter, or to her dogs.

Charlotte Mailliard Swig

She is San Francisco's chief of protocol and her husband owns the Fairmont Hotel chain; she once threw a party on the Golden Gate Bridge and a million people came; she is constantly in the news and the mayor calls her regularly, but this woman takes it all in stride. Only Charlotte Mailliard Swig, one of San Francisco's most beloved personalities, would name her cocker spaniel Stevie Wonderful.

Stevie greets visitors in Barbara Bush pearls as the dignified houseman opens the door to the Swigs' spectacular penthouse apartment surrounded with soaring floor-to-ceiling windows overlooking the Bay. The apartment, just one of the Swigs' many residences, is extraordinary – it is like floating on a cloud of soft peaches and creams in the middle of the ocean. It is hard to tell where the ocean ends and the sky begins, and even the gourmet kitchen is blessed with panoramic views of the Golden Gate Bridge and beyond. The furnishings are antique, the floors marble, the fabrics muted, and masses of pink tulips spill out of celadon vases everywhere.

Stevie rushes up the circular staircase that emanates from the center of this tremendous room that comprises the entry hall, the living room, and the dining room. Her owner appears at the top of the stairs in a beaded ball gown, and Mrs. Swig's native Texas charm is immediately evident. "Oh, I see you've met Stevie," she says, extending her hand in a no-nonsense handshake. "Aren't dogs so wonderful?" She sweeps up Stevie and adds, "They love you even if you're overdrawn."

Mrs. Swig is quite humorous as she explains her affinity for cocker spaniels (of which she has three). "I started the cockers in this town," she says. "I've given one to (former mayor) Dianne Feinstein; my doctor has one; my doctor's daughter has one; I've given them to everyone. We are the cocker connection!"

To honor her favorite breed, Mrs. Swig has initiated a "cocker core" parade in the town of Sonoma. Its participants include many of Stevie's closest relatives, all wearing special dog visors. Stevie's popularity is enhanced by her custom of giving over 50 presents to her dog friends every Christmas. Last year she gave doggie deer antlers (Millie Bush got pearls). In years past her gifts have included *Dogue* magazine and Georgio for Dogs, and, like her owner, Stevie is renowned for her parties. While entertaining Sandy, the canine star of *Annie*, Stevie once had a fireplug delivered to the fourth floor, and she has graciously entertained "many heads of state."

As Mrs. Swig and her "most beautiful girl in the world" begin to pose for their photograph, a perfect rainbow appears over the Bay. The scene could not be more spectacular – the rainbow matches perfectly the sparkling rainbow hues of Mrs. Swig's gown and enhances the apartment's rainbow-toned decor. Charlotte Swig could brighten up any cloudy day.

Ivana Trump

*I*vana Trump is not only glamorous and gorgeous, she is a dog lover as well. She grew up with dogs in her native Czechoslovakia and now shares her Trump Tower triplex penthouse with a two-year-old black toy poodle, Tiapka.

Tiapka is actually Tiapka II; the first Tiapka was the black poodle that Ivana had for 14 years. When that poodle was a "tiny puppy," she fell and hurt her paw, and that is how she came to be named Tiapka, which is Czech for "paw." Tiapka II, whose nickname is Choppy, "comes from a line of champions and loves to eat grapes," says Ivana.

Choppy spends most of his time with Ivana's three children and sleeps with her daughter Ivanka. He gets up when she does and has his own breakfast while the children are eating theirs, and then the children play with him before dressing and going to school. Ivana's description of Choppy's day is, "Once the children are off, their nanny takes Choppy out on our garden rooftop, where he runs and plays for hours. He comes in during the afternoon and usually naps before the children return home. Then it's just a matter of whose attention he can get first, what devilish little tricks come next."

Choppy has many tricks up his paw, and one of his favorites is, as the family is preparing to leave town, sneaking into the gray suitcase that Ivana's mother always carries. "Instead of running around trying to make sure he is noticed and not left home alone," says Ivana, "Choppy just finds this gray bag and sits on it. He knows Grandma won't leave home without it!" Choppy has obviously inherited some of his owner's intelligence.

Tanya Tucker

anya Tucker looks too young to be a country music legend, but since she belted out "Delta Dawn" at age 14 she has had over 30 Top Ten songs, half of which made it to number one. "The Texas Tornado" has racked up an astonishing 16 hit records in a row and shows no sign of slowing down. In 1991 Tanya has played over 200 dates, breaking attendance records everywhere, has made numerous television appearances, and has won the National Cutting Horse Association's Annual Futurity Celebrity Cutting Championship. On her cross-country tours, Tanya is always accompanied by her baby daughter, Presley, and her adored bishon frisé, Lucy.

Tanya's photo shoot is taking place in a Fort Worth Holiday Inn where the husky-voiced singer is getting ready for her appearance at the famed western bar, Billy Bob's. She is due onstage in one hour but sits calmly praising her canine companion in her hotel suite surrounded by four of her friends, their husbands and assorted band members. Tanya always has time for this very important member of the Tucker family. Lucy, who has appeared on two album covers, travels everywhere with Tanya, by bus, air and car; but her airplane trips have recently been curtailed as Lucy has developed a fear of flying.

Lucy was given to Tanya by Glen Campbell 11 years ago, when he bought the puppy at a mall in South Carolina. When she's not traveling, this white bundle of fur lives with Tanya in Nashville, where Lucy's favorite activity is playing in the water at Old Hickory Lake. She and Tanya are kindred spirits. "Lucy immediately picks up on whatever mood I'm in," says Tanya. "If I'm sad or happy, so is she. She is my shadow."

As her curtain time draws near, Tanya, who is a complete professional, casually mentions that she had better start thinking about what she's going to wear onstage. As she's walking into the room with her elaborate wardrobe, she's asked if Lucy likes music and answers that she does. What kind? "She's partial to my music," says the star.

Blair Underwood

lair Underwood never needs to worry about having any unexpected visitors at his beautifully decorated Hollywood Hills home. The "L.A. Law" star is more than guarded by his two massive German shepherds, Shaka and Kinga, and friends would be wise to call before arriving. Shaka, (the word means "leader" or "warrior" in Swahili) and Kinga ("protector") are aptly named. Both dogs are extremely possessive of their owner. "I chose shepherds because they are big and look mean but are actually very loving," says the handsome star who plays lawyer Jonathan Rollins on the hit series. Also, he had grown up with German shepherds, and, as a self-described "Army brat," had lived in Germany and could master the German commands to which these highly trained dogs respond.

As Blair and his "babies" are being photographed in Laurel Canyon's famed "Dog Park," he is wearing weight-training gloves. The reason for these gloves is soon evident when a perky poodle strolls by and his two massive shep-

herds literally pull Blair up out of his seat – the dogs pretend not to hear their owner's repeated command of "Nein," and Blair jokes that he is a lot stronger since Shaka and Kinga have entered his life.

Blair is trying to coax his spectacular shepherds back into his little sports car, when a man walking a rather motley mixed-breed comments on how beautiful Blair's dogs are. Ever the nice guy, Blair graciously thanks the man and, looking at his seriously unattractive dog, replies, "Now that's a beautiful dog you have there, too." All dogs are beautiful in their own way, but Blair Underwood is a gentleman beyond compare.

The photo shoot has been successful until Kinga, getting a little overly excited about all the other dogs in the parking lot, wets the leg of Blair's publicist, Felice. Blair remains undaunted. "Anything that has to do with dogs, I don't mind," he says. Hopefully Felice feels the same way.

Joan Van Ark

The living room of Joan Van Ark's Mulholland Drive home is abuzz with excitement as a huge bundle of fur bounds through the front door. Joan, "Knots Landing's" Valene Ewing Gibson, named her Old English sheepdog for the town of Boulder, Colorado, where he came from. The name Boulder is most appropriate.

Joan was in Colorado doing a charity benefit when she first saw the cuddly puppy. She says, "My husband, Jack, just looked at me and said, 'No, positively not,' but twenty-four hours later, there we were buying a flea collar."

Joan has never been able to resist animals, and because of her five cats, Boulder is usually relegated to his kennel outside, overlooking the canyons. (Joan says he has the best view in town.) Joan and the sheepdog have a "little chat" every day when she goes to her outdoor spa, and he sometimes runs with his owner, but, as Joan is a hard-core athlete, Boulder finds it a little exhausting. He prefers his twice-daily romps with Joan's housekeeper.

Street-smart Joan contrasts noticeably with her naive and eager-to-please pet, but they do have one thing in common. Joan and Boulder both have their hair blown-dry every morning – it seems the two share a penchant for high-maintenance dos.

Eddie Velez

Repo Man and *Romero* star Eddie Velez bought three Siberian Huskies "because he wanted something to play with." Now he has his hands full with Blue Bandit, a two-year-old; Red Bandit, the puppy; and Dino, named for Dean Martin. The rowdiness of Eddie's dogs belies his own quiet and distinguished manner.

As he puffs on his omnipresent cigar, this busy movie and TV actor explains that he loves the Huskies' energy because he "didn't want dogs that just sat around." With each of these three it was "love at first sight," and he does not plan to stop here. He claims, "I intend to have at least six Huskies and take them up to Alaska where they can pull me around in a sled." The Velez household will never recover.

Jack Wagner

Jack Wagner might be a heartthrob to his adoring female fans, but to his golden retrievers, Elvis and Suzy, this fact is of little consequence. Jack's fame as Frisco Jones on "General Hospital," his new role as Warren Lockridge on "Santa Barbara," and his flourishing recording career do not impress the dogs; they care more about his ability to throw a mean tennis ball.

Every teenage female in America would love to trade places with the retrievers as they frolic in the park with the multitalented young star, risquély clad in strategically torn jeans. With his customary quick wit, Jack vetoes having the dogs photographed next to a Beverly Hills fire engine, saying, "We've only lived in Beverly Hills four days, and I'm not ready for the dogs to acquire that attitude."

Jack, who went to the top of the charts with his hit single "All I Need," named his dog Elvis because the retriever also likes to sing. Suzy is named Suzy rather than Priscilla because "it's not a family deal."

The dogs' indifference to Jack's appearance is evidenced when the group is leaving. As the driver gets into the car, both dogs hop into the front seat, leaving Jack to climb into the back. No, they are definitely not impressed.

Rick Wallace & David Kelley

*I*n a quaint little ivy-covered cottage that feels a million miles away from Hollywood, one of the most critically acclaimed television shows of all time is written and produced. Amazingly enough, this serene setting is smack dab in the middle of the massive Twentieth Century Fox lot, and the two blue-jean-clad preppy-looking kids throwing Frisbees with their dogs happen to be the executive producers of "L.A. Law."

Rick Wallace and David Kelley are unexpected as this industry's boy-wonder team. They are young, laid-back, and it is not at all surprising to find that they bring their dogs to work with them every morning. Hughie, Rick's 9-year-old sheltie, even gets driven to work when Rick is out of town. She occupies herself by playing with the dogs of other "L.A. Law" staff members, including Hogan, David's "Labradoodle." Kelley explains that in his Maine hometown, his Labrador "jumped the fence with a standard poodle," and Hogan, the fine product of that union, was born in his family's backyard.

Kelley, appropriately enough, practiced law in Boston for three years before joining the "L.A. Law" team. During his brief but spectacular career with the program, he has won three Emmys and ten nominations and used his legal expertise and quick wit to write a majority of the show's episodes.

Rick, a Chicago native who directed several episodes of "Hill Street Blues," has been with "L.A. Law" since its debut five years ago and has directed many episodes. He says he "loves all creatures," as does David, who always carries around a pocketful of Pupperonis. Both of these multi-talented young men seem to share their dogs' mellow personalities, but fortunately Hughie and Hogan do not totally emulate their owners. Rick claims to be thankful that Hughie doesn't share his more excessive personality traits. "If Hughie was like me," jokes the two-time Emmy winner, "she'd be running around with an Uzi."

Andy Warhol

Betty White

It's nine o'clock Sunday morning and, after a glamorous evening accepting a Golden Globe award, actress Betty White is relentlessly surveying the backyard of her hillside home, pooper-scooper in hand. No retinue waits on this gracious lady, a five-time Emmy winner who is as famous for her intense love of animals as she is for her leading roles – as happy homemaker Sue Ann Nivens in "The Mary Tyler Moore Show" and currently, as naive Rose in "The Golden Girls." Betty is crazy about animals in general, her own three dogs in particular.

"My dogs have pulled me through a lot," says this tireless worker who lost her beloved husband, "Password" host Allen Ludden, in 1981. This champion of animal rights considers her role as president of the Morris Animal Foundation her real job and her TV show her hobby. Betty reflects the thoughts of many successful celebrities when she claims that a pet is the "one person you can trust completely."

The White menagerie includes Dinah, an elderly golden retriever who was recently retired as blind actor Tom Sullivan's guide dog, and the "boys": Timmy, a ten-year-old poodle, and Cricket, a "near-miss bichon frisé." Although all three dogs share Betty's bed, they, like their owner, lead a comparatively unassuming life. No Tinseltown glitter for this troupe that eats regular dog food and splurges on basic store-bought biscuits.

Their days are spent resting in preparation for Betty's evening arrival, although Dinah, the retired guide dog, has not forgotten her intense training. She is constantly handing Betty her slippers and picking up anything dropped. Her proud owner brags, "Dinah is so bright – anything you ask of her, she does." Betty is currently writing a book highlighting Dinah's incredible achievements. She has already written one book extolling the virtues of pet ownership.

There is not a bad word to be said in Hollywood about this generous woman who handwrites her own thank-you notes and works tirelessly for her causes. She came by her love of animals naturally or, as she puts it, "in the womb," and she has devoted her life to protecting animals, trying to give back a little of what they've given her. As Betty hugs her three pets to her, she wistfully adds, "I do feel sorry for people who aren't into animals – they are missing so much."

Mollie Wilmot

Mollie "Mercedes" Wilmot's Palm Beach backyard where an Argentine tanker ship landed.

Canines

Benji & Joe Camp

Photo by Mulberry Square Productions©

*I*n a world of gifted dogs, one stands alone. Benji is not only sharp and intuitive, but a heck of an actor as well.

"Benji is the most educated and has the best vocabulary of any dog that's ever lived," says his owner Joe Camp, who created the "Benji" character and wrote all the Benji movies.

This movie star, who is actually Benji II (the original Benji's daughter), can follow a wide variety of instructions as complicated as swimming underwater in specially made scuba-diving gear. Camp insists that "Benji knows when

she's acting, and she knows what it means to 'feel' one way or another."

Benji is being handsomely rewarded for her hard work, and she recently became the first animal to command residuals – payments made for repeated airings of a show. When she is not working, Benji sleeps in bed between her trainer Frank Inn and Frank's wife Juanita, and participates in basic dog activities. The only difference, says Joe, is that "when other dogs are learning how to sit or stay, Benji is learning how to look sad or happy."

Buck

"Married...With Children" star Buck is quite the dog about town these days. He has starred in the film *Scrooged*, a multitude of commercials, and he even has an appearance in Janet Jackson's "When I Think of You" music video, but none of this has gone to his head. The six-year-old briard remains his calm, sensitive self.

His owner and trainer, Steve Ritt, says Buck looks forward to going to work, and that everybody on the set, especially star Ed O'Neill, spends a lot of time playing with him. What does this particular shaggy dog have that has skyrocketed him to fame and fortune? His owner lists Buck's two main skills as yawning and kissing – the requirements for being a dog star are obviously amazingly similar to those required of human stars.

Dreyfuss & Richard Mulligan

Although it's said that every dog has his day, it's not every dog who has his own television show. Dreyfuss, the 110-pound combination Saint Bernard and golden retriever who stars in "Empty Nest," recently had his own episode in which he intervened in a family dispute. Now that's stardom.

Gary Jacobs, executive producer for "Empty Nest," has said, "From the letters and the audience response we get, it's evident Dreyfuss is one of our most popular characters." This is quite a compliment considering the enormous popularity of this show, which always places in the top ten in the ratings.

The star's owner, Gary Gero, has always been an animal lover and makes sure Dreyfuss gets the best care possible. Aside from dog food, Dreyfuss eats fruit and vegetables, and steak is his special treat. "He likes nothing better than a piece of good lean meat," says Gero.

Dreyfuss, whose real name is Bear, is from a show-biz background. His mother, Molly, was recently in *Steel Magnolias* and his father, Boomer, was in "Father Murphy" and *Summer Rental*. The five-year-old Southern California native is very intelligent, but his best trick is "playing dumb," and in real life Dreyfuss is a bit high-strung – quite a switch from his chronically laid-back "Empty Nest" character. Now who says dogs can't act?

Lassie

No book on top dogs would be complete without the most famous dog of them all, Lassie. At the height of her illustrious career, in the 1950s, this star reigned supreme at MGM and commanded a $5,000-a-week salary, matched only by MGM's other most beautiful star, Elizabeth Taylor. Today, Lassie's seventh-generation descendant is back on the air.

The current Lassie stars on a show aptly titled, "The New Lassie," and is trained by famed animal trainer Robert Weatherwax, the son of the man who trained the original Lassie 40 years ago. Weatherwax says Lassie is extremely smart and can be taught all sorts of things. "With Lassie almost anything is possible," says the trainer. "One of his most humorous habits is that when he goes into his bedroom to take a nap, he closes the door behind him."

Lassie, who really is a he instead of a she, knows more than 150 commands and works from 7:00 a.m. to 6:30 p.m. five days a week. He doesn't seem to mind this grueling schedule – possibly because he gets a doughnut every morning when he gets to the set and snacks on boiled beef throughout the day "to keep his energy level up" – but more likely because stardom is in his blood.

Rin Tin Tin

The real story of Rin Tin Tin started back in 1918 when an Allied Air Force gunner found a little puppy huddling in a bombed-out enemy trench and crawled back to the Allied side with this puppy and his sister in tow. The soldier, Lee Duncan, named the puppy Rin Tin Tin and brought him home to California when the war was over.

He and Rin Tin Tin were discovered by a movie director one day as they were out on a walk, and soon mega-producer Darryl Zanuck had Rin Tin Tin under contract for his first movie, *Where the North Begins*. The noble and beautiful German shepherd then starred in more than 27 movies, and in 1932 was the biggest box office star in America, receiving top billing in all his films.

In 1954, producer Herbert Leonard decided to do a television series featuring one of the original Rin Tin Tin's descendants, and he produced 164 episodes of a show that, according to his publicist, "had every kid in America wanting a Rin Tin Tin." Today, Rin Tin Tin's name lives on as the same producer, Herbert Leonard, 38 years later is now producing television's "Rin Tin Tin, K-9 Cop." The canine legend lives on, and Rin Tin Tin is still getting top billing.

National Dog Institute Motto

To educate and inform people all over the world that
they never have to punish their dogs again.

That hurting, hitting, yelling, or dominating the dog in
any way is wrong.

That there is a much better way, a kinder, more
humane method of training.

The *Matthew Margolis Method* of love, praise, and
affection training will enable people everywhere to
have the ultimate pet, friend,
and protector.

Animal Protection Groups

Actors and Others for Animals
5510 Cahuenga Blvd.
North Hollywood, CA 91501
(818) 985-6263

Humane Society of the United States
2100 L Street N.W.
Washington, DC 20037
(202) 452-1100

Morris Animal Foundation
45 Inverness Drive East
Englewood, CO 80112
(303) 790-1067

People for the Ethical Treatment of Animals
P.O. Box 42516
Washington, DC 20015
(301) 770-PETA

Friends of Animals
National Headquarters
P. O. Box 1244
Norwalk, Connecticut 06856
(203) 866-5223

Photo Credits

TOP DOG Creators

Bonnie Skinner Levy, John Haynsworth, Liz Walker, and their TOP DOGS.

Bill Blass Lesli... Joan Embery Roger Horchu... Georgette Klinger Liza Min...

...gdale George Bush Michael Douglas Earl Holliman Bill Kirchenbauer Jayne Meadows Ronald Reagan Marina Sir...

...t Dole Heloise Mrs. Francis A. Martin T. Boone Pickens Richard Simmons Bl...

David Hasselhoff David Kelley Michelle Pfeiffer Bobby Short Ivana Trump Tanya Tucker Buck...

Daniel Kapavik Garry Marshall Mollie Wilmot Benji

Matthew Margolis Mrs. Allen Paulson Marge Schott Charlotte Swig Betsy Bloomingda...

Michael Paré Dina Schmidt Sally Struthers Betty White Bill Blass David Hasselho...

Jack Scalia Andy Warhol Bijan Daniel Kapavik

...bach Jimmy Stewart Rick Wallace David Bates Armand Deutsch Matthew Marg...

Jack Wagner Jimmy Barker Victor Costa Ed Cox Harris Katleman Mrs.

...ay Ash Lucille Ball Gary Collins Mrs. Earle Jorgensen Bob Mackie Michael Paré Dina S...

Nat King Cole John James Liberace Jack Nicholson Jack Scalia

Jacobs Barbara Lazaroff Moore Roehm Jimmy Stewart

...ohn...